The Souls of
W. E. B. Du Bois

Great Barrington Books

Bringing the old and new together
in the spirit of W. E. B. Du Bois

~ An imprint edited by Charles Lemert ~

Titles Available

Keeping Good Time: Reflections on Knowledge, Power, and People
by Avery F. Gordon (2004)

Going Down for Air: A Memoir in Search of a Subject
by Derek Sayer (2004)

The Souls of Black Folk,
100th Anniversary Edition
by W. E. B. Du Bois, with commentaries by Manning Marable,
Charles Lemert, and Cheryl Townsend Gilkes (2004)

Sociology After the Crisis, Updated Edition
by Charles Lemert (2004)

Subject to Ourselves
by Anthony Elliot (2004)

The Protestant Ethic Turns 100:
Essays on the Centenary of the Weber Thesis
edited by William H. Swatos, Jr., and Lutz Kaelber (2005)

Seeing Sociologically: The Routine Grounds of Social Action
by Harold Garfinkel, edited and introduced by Anne Warfield Rawls (2005)

Discourses on Liberation: An Anatomy of Critical Theory
by Kyung-Man Kim (2005)

The Souls of W. E. B. Du Bois
by Alford A. Young, Jr., Manning Marable, Elizabeth Higginbotham,
Charles Lemert, and Jerry G. Watts (2006)

Forthcoming
Radical Nomad: C. Wright Mills and His Times
by Tom Hayden with Contemporary Reflections by Stanley Aronowitz,
Richard Flacks, and Charles Lemert

Thinking the Unthinkable:
An Introduction to Social Theories
by Charles Lemert

Critique for What? Cultural Studies, American Studies, Left Studies
by Joel Pfister

Everyday Life and the State
by Peter Bratsis

The Souls of
W. E. B. Du Bois

*by Alford A. Young, Jr., Manning Marable,
Elizabeth Higginbotham, Charles Lemert,
and Jerry G. Watts*

Paradigm Publishers
Boulder • London

Copyright © 2006 by Paradigm Publishers

Chapter 1 originally appeared as the introduction to *The Souls of Black Folk, 100th Anniversary Edition* by W. E. B. Du Bois, with commentaries by Manning Marable, Charles Lemert, and Cheryl Townsend Gilkes. Copyright © 2004 by Paradigm Publishers.

Published in the United States by Paradigm Publishers, 3360 Mitchell Lane, Suite E, Boulder, Colorado 80301 USA.

Paradigm Publishers is the trade name of Birkenkamp & Company, LLC, Dean Birkenkamp, President and Publisher.

Library of Congress Cataloging-in-Publication Data has been applied for.

ISBN 1-59451-137-3 (hardcover: alk. paper)
ISBN 1-59451-138-1 (pbk.: alk. paper)

Printed and bound in the United States of America on acid-free paper that meets the standards of the American National Standard for Permanence of Paper for Printed Library Materials.

Designed and Typeset by Straight Creek Bookmakers.

10 09 08 07 06
1 2 3 4 5

Contents

Introduction

Alford A. Young, Jr.

Today, slightly more than one hundred years since the publication of his classic work *The Souls of Black Folk,* it may not seem surprising if some are compelled to say out loud, "What more is there to say about W. E. B. Du Bois and this great work?" In fact, despite some efforts to say more about Du Bois and that scholarly endeavor, there still remains much that is unsaid, or at least understated, about *The Souls of Black Folk.* Some of what should be said concerns the extent to which Du Bois strove to generate a conversation not only with a broader audience in academia and the American public but also within and across his own body of scholarship, where *Souls* stands as a centerpiece. Accordingly, what needs to be said, debated, and advanced concerns the means by which Du Bois called upon the research and analytical tools available at the time of his writing, regardless of whether they fit neatly within a social scientific or humanities canon, to explore and extrapolate upon the situation of black Americans in the nascent industrial hegemon that was the United States at the beginning of the twentieth century. *The Souls of Black Folk* was a heroic effort to address this concern by providing a pivotal commentary that was spun toward a range of issues, concerns, and questions such that one has to consider *Souls* not only as a document of great internal sophistication but also as one that reaches out to other parts of Du Bois's scholarship and other parts of his professional life. While some books have been written about Du Bois and his efforts concerning *The Souls of Black Folk,* rarely has it been the case that a complete volume aims to vigorously explore the relationship of *Souls* to Du Bois's other writings at the beginning of the twentieth century. *The Souls of W. E. B. Du Bois* aims to do

---

Each author follows his or her preference regarding the capitalization of *black* and *white* in this book.

1

that very work. It is a collection of essays exploring the relationship of W. E. B. Du Bois's seminal publication, *The Souls of Black Folk*, to other works in his scholarly portfolio and to his personal project concerning race, racial identity, and the social objectives of scholarly engagement.

The Souls of Black Folk is often taken, and quite legitimately so, as a stand-alone publication elucidating Du Bois's turn-of-the-century thinking about the existential foundations of the African American community and the African American social condition. Yet, *Souls* also serves as one of a series of critical commentaries by Du Bois on these and other themes. As the authors of *The Souls of W. E. B. Du Bois* demonstrate, these commentaries are in conversation with each other. Hence, rather than providing internal critiques of the ideas and arguments introduced in *Souls,* the essays in this book offer pointed assessments of how *Souls* extends, refines, or intro- duces ideas considered in Du Bois's *The Philadelphia Negro* and *Black Reconstruction* and of how *Souls* relates to Du Bois's early considerations of social activism on the behalf of African Americans and to his thinking about the situation of African American women. A little more than one hundred years after the publication of *The Souls of Black Folk,* these essays demonstrate how significant *Souls* is for Du Bois's overarching objectives concerning racial theorizing, the social conditions affecting African Americans at the turn of the century, and the possibilities for social justice.

One of the most compelling aspects of *The Souls of Black Folk* is the very title of the work. Du Bois's use of the term *souls* compels one to think about what it means to be a black American (whether the reader happens to occupy that status or not), and the experience of reading that work also motivates one to think about how Du Bois took stock of his own situation as a black American. Each of the essays in *The Souls of W. E. B. Du Bois* employs or emphasizes some notion of soul in developing its argument. In most cases, this is done by exploring how Du Bois's soul (or, to put it in other words, his sense of self) lingers throughout his work on projects aside from the writing of *The Souls of Black Folk*. Hence, the title of this book, *The Souls of W. E. B. Du Bois,* is a reference to both the relationship of Du Bois's other works to his classic text, *The Souls of Black Folk,* and the relationship of Du Bois's inner sense of self to his political and intellectual pursuits.

This collection of essays that comprise *The Souls of W. E. B. Du Bois* first came together at the calling of Charles Lemert, who, with

Alford A. Young, Jr., assembled a session at the American Sociological Association Annual Meeting in Atlanta, Georgia, in August 2003. That session, entitled "W. E. B. Du Bois and the Souls of Sociology: A Century of Cultural Uncertainty," included presentations by Lemert and Young and by fellow contributors Elizabeth Higginbotham and Jerry G. Watts. A little over a year later, in September 2004, these four scholars reassembled to present revised essays on their respective topics and engage in a panel-style discussion at the 2004 Matthew Lemert Memorial Lecture Series at Wesleyan University. In the year subsequent to the gathering at Wesleyan University, these authors completed their work on their respective chapters.

The final contributor to *The Souls of W. E. B. Du Bois,* Manning Marable, was brought into the project due to his long-standing involvement in studying W. E. B. Du Bois as both a scholar and a social activist. While Marable's chapter is a reprinted version of his introduction to a hundredth-anniversary edition of *The Souls of Black Folk* (Du Bois 2004), it deserves a place in this work as it bridges those chapters that emphasize Du Bois's scholarly agenda with those that explore his more activist dispositions and inclinations.

The Souls of W. E. B. Du Bois begins with Marable's chapter on the intellectual and practical political implications of the publication of *The Souls of Black Folk.* Here Marable delivers a provocative assessment of how *Souls* was read in its time of production and at various points up to the present. Included in this commentary is consideration of how Du Bois, himself, responded to his work in the decades following its release.

In the second chapter Elizabeth Higginbotham argues that Du Bois wrestled with how to portray and interpret the agency of African American women when it was often coupled with some faulty notion of sexuality as the cornerstone feature of such agency. She asserts that Du Bois was daring in his effort to assess not only the suffering that black women encountered as a marginalized element of American society but also the role of black women in the economic spheres of black America and American society more generally and the unique challenges they faced and the actions they pursued on the behalf of family and community interest.

The third chapter, by Alford A. Young, Jr., provides a literary analysis of *The Philadelphia Negro* as a work that, for various reasons, begins to do the problematic work that is more fully pursued in *Souls.* Young aims to demonstrate how *The Philadelphia Negro* reflects the soul of W. E. B. Du Bois in that it sheds much light on the ways in which Du Bois tried to make sense of what it must have felt like to be a black American near the beginning of the twentieth century. As Young states, many aspects of that feeling are beyond the purview of formal social scientific inquiry to grasp and interpret. Yet, while being aware of this, Du Bois pushed that objective as far as he could in *The Philadelphia Negro*. Young maintains that reading *The Souls of Black Folk* is essential for fully comprehending the boundaries and limits of *The Philadelphia Negro*'s efforts to achieve this end.

The fourth chapter, by Charles Lemert, examines the political ramifications of the cultural analysis put forth by Du Bois in a series of his works ranging from *The Souls of Black Folk* to his 1935 publication *Black Reconstruction*. Professor Lemert explores what it meant for Du Bois to be an intellectual, or cultural agent, in his time and what bearing and relationship this had on black intellectuals (African as well as African American) of later periods who aspired to link intellectual pursuits with an agenda for practical political transformation. In this chapter, Lemert deftly captures how Du Bois worked both within and ahead of his time in his effort to carve out spaces for black intellectual immersion into politically relevant change through the medium of cultural analysis.

The fifth and final chapter, by Jerry G. Watts, explores issues similar to those considered by Lemert. Yet rather than emphasize Du Bois's contemporaneous and farsighted orientation embraced by Lemert, Watts privileges Du Bois's struggle to function as both a member of and a figure far out ahead of the African American community. Watts explores the tensions that Du Bois encountered in trying to function as an intellectual who should not have to be encumbered by his classification in a devalued racial category. In doing so, Watts also explores how Du Bois strove to be a responsible intellectual and social critic and therefore had to confront his inclusion into that category and the possibilities (however remote at his time) for improving both the conditions bearing upon African Americans and their public image in the minds of many Americans. Watts points to *The Souls of Black Folk* as a central publication for exploring how Du Bois grappled with these circumstances and tensions. Essentially, Watts's emphasis on the social contexts of the within and ahead-of locations of Du Bois as an intellectual and scholar offers an appropriate and intriguing parallel to Lemert's temporal contextualization of within and ahead-of.

The essays in this volume, especially the contributions by Jerry G. Watts and Manning Marable, deliver lucid assessments of what *Souls* offers as a supradisciplinary approach toward discerning the African American social and existential condition. The analytical coherence of *Souls* is much more comprehensible when the work is taken as a text that spans the social sciences and the humanities. As Watts and Marable also demonstrate, the shortcomings and inadequacies of *The Souls of Black Folk* are also better grasped by employing that kind of analytical lens.

The collection of essays in *The Souls of W. E. B. Du Bois* indicates that much more, indeed, can be said about Du Bois; *The Souls of Black Folk*; Du Bois's scholarly portfolio more generally; and Du Bois's work in the area of civil rights, political change, and social transformation. In short, these chapters affirm that anyone who truly believes that no more need be said about Du Bois is wholly unequipped to think seriously about the status and significance of race in modern times, the lingering conditions of social inequality, and the possibilities for intellectual service to the cause of ameliorating these situations. In that sense, the authors have come together in this book with the aspiration of generating new thinking about one of Du Bois's works that is both a classic commentary about the past and an instrument for assessing the present and possible future of the African American social condition and the interconnection of politics and scholarship.

1

Celebrating Souls
Deconstructing the Du Boisian Legacy

Manning Marable

It was unquestionably the social event of the year. Even one reporter from the *Detroit News* characterized the audience that evening as being "splendidly attired."[1] There were thousands of well-groomed black men striking poses in tuxedos and dark business suits. Thousands of African American women graced the auditorium in splendid evening gowns and sparkling jewelry. The vast Cobo Hall, Detroit's largest indoor arena, was literally overflowing with the elite group once described by W. E. B. Du Bois as the "Talented Tenth"—the most affluent, best-educated sector of black America. On the evening of April 27, 2003, more than eight thousand people paid a minimum of $150.00 each to attend the Detroit chapter of the National Association for the Advancement of Colored People's (NAACP) "Fight for Freedom Fund Dinner." At the central dais—the Cobo Arena was so cavernous that there were actually four daises—were seated Michigan's governor, one senator, several congressmen, the chief executive officer of Daimler Chrysler Corporation, and the nation's leading hip-hop mogul, Russell Simmons. The purpose of the night's historic celebration was to mark the one-hundredth anniversary of the publication of *The Souls of Black Folk*, by William Edward Burghardt Du Bois. The gala's organizers, planning carefully to make sure that Du Bois's celebrated text was at the center of the festivities, placed a complimentary copy of *The Souls of Black Folk* at each individual place setting.

As the evening's keynote speaker, I had been assigned the task of explaining, over the clatter of silverware and the background music of the Motown sound, the central ideas advanced by Du Bois in his classic work, and linking the book's significance to the particular challenges confronting black Americans in the twenty-first century. From my vantage point on the dais, sitting next to Russell Simmons, I couldn't help but reflect on black history's many ironies. Representatives of corporate America and transnational capitalism were prominently present that evening to finance what the Detroit press proudly announced was the "largest sit-down banquet" in the country. Du Bois was repeatedly projected in the local Detroit media as among the pantheon of America's greatest thinkers and as the political architect of the Civil Rights Movement. Few in the audience probably knew that in 1951 the U.S. Justice Department had arrested and tried Du Bois unsuccessfully on the grounds of being an unlicensed representative of a foreign power, namely the Soviet Union. During the "Great Fear" of McCarthyism, *The Souls of Black Folk* and other works by Du Bois were frequently removed from libraries as examples of Communist-inspired propaganda. Black America's poet laureate Langston Hughes, after giving humiliating witness before Senator Joseph McCarthy's subcommittee, removed Du Bois from a revised edition of *Famous American Negroes*. At the public celebration of Du Bois's ninetieth birthday in 1958, which attracted an audience of over one thousand at New York's Roosevelt Hotel, the NAACP chose not to sponsor the event. The hostility and fear once attached to Du Bois's name were still so strong that even at the moment of his death on August 27, 1963, he remained highly problematic to the mainstream leadership of the Civil Rights Movement. Indeed, at the historic August 28, 1963, March on Washington, D.C., NAACP leader Roy Wilkins announced Du Bois's recent demise to the mass demonstration, emphasizing "the fact that in his later years Dr. Du Bois chose another path."[2]

Wilkins's words of admonition were either forgotten or ignored forty years later by a new generation of NAACP leaders at *The Souls of Black Folk* centennial celebration. Yet the gala event occurred at the same time that U.S. troops had launched a military invasion of Iraq, a Third World conflict Du Bois certainly would have opposed. The celebration occurred as the Bush Administration aggressively sought to quell domestic protest and civil dissent by implementing measures of the Patriot Act—provisions that possibly would have defined an activist like Du Bois as a "subversive." Little of this, however, was part of the orchestrated agenda for the evening, aside from my own remarks. Other speakers, in a mantra of repetition, framed their acknowledgements of Du Bois's greatness around two key phrases, both drawn from *Souls*: that the "Negro is a sort of seventh son, born with a veil" and gifted with a "double conscious-ness" or a kind of "two-ness—an American, a Negro; two souls, two thoughts, two unreconciled strivings ...";and that the "problem of the twentieth century is the problem of the color-line."

The official literature produced for the occasion offered little in the way of interpretation concerning the lasting significance of *Souls* and its relationship to contemporary African American issues. In the banquet brochure, "*The Souls of Black Folk*: 100 Years Later," Detroit Mayor Kwame Kilpatrick suggested that the dinner's theme was truly relevant in 2003, as "African-Americans continue to face many of the same challenges our community faced a century ago." The lessons of *Souls* and the continuing work of the NAACP were dedicated to encouraging "all people of color to work together to level the playing field and ensure equal opportunity for everyone." More complex and also problematic was the statement of congratu-lations from Kweisi Mfume, NAACP president and chief executive officer. "Du Bois's epic work described aspects of an existence too often unrecognized or regarded without sympathy by the majority of Americans a century ago," Mfume observed. "He also offered empathy for those who oppressed African-Americans, even while describing the cruelties committed due to the divisiveness of the color-line." Mfume's curious construction made Du Bois seem more like Martin Luther King, Jr., than the author of *Souls*. The real goal of Du Bois, according to Mfume, was the achievement of "mutual respect ... as a necessary prelude to harmonious coexistence" be-tween racial groups. Du Bois "reviled" racial hatred, "but not those who espoused or acted upon it. Our association's commitment to its mission of enlightenment, empowerment, and peaceful integration has not strayed, and for all our setbacks, much has been gained."[3] Thus fifty-five years after he was fired from the NAACP, and forty years after his death in involuntary exile in Ghana, both Du Bois and his most famous text are comfortably reassimilated into the current mission statement of the civil rights establishment.

I couldn't help but wonder what Du Bois himself would have thought about this multimillion-dollar fête in his honor. Being the careful social scientist that he was, Du Bois would probably ask what was really being celebrated. There was certainly a superficial familiarity with passages from *Souls* by most of the evening's speakers, but virtually no mention of the repressive, brutal context of life under Jim Crow segregation in the South that was the immediate environment for the writing of this collection of essays. The metaphor of the "color-line" provided useful connections with the realities of structural racism in the post–civil rights era—the continuing burdens black Americans endure in the form of lower life expectancies, higher infant mortality rates, lower rates of college enrollment and graduation, and high rates of imprisonment. Then, sitting high above the Talented Tenth, I finally understood the deeper meaning of the celebration. Du Bois had given the emerging black middle class a lyrical language of racial reform. *Souls* was to the black American petit bourgeoisie what *The Communist Manifesto* had once been for sectors of the European proletariat under industrial capitalism in the late nineteenth cenutury: a framework for understanding history, a philosophical statement establishing group identity and social location within society's unequal hierarchy, and an appeal for collective action and resistance to oppression and exploitation. But the black elite, and its corporate sponsors, weren't interested in "class struggle" or in Du Bois's Marxist politics after World War II. The black elite was there largely to celebrate itself and the general advancement of the race within U.S. society as it exists. Du Bois was being honored for giving that rising class a language of its own.

The Detroit NAACP chapter's massive celebration of *Souls* was the largest single event of its kind during the book's centennial year, but there were at least several hundred other such public programs. The most ambitious was sponsored by the National Black Arts Festival in Atlanta, July 18–27, 2003. Its self-described mission of "Searching for Soul ... in all the right places" coyly combined the "spotlight on W. E. B. Du Bois" with a wide-ranging series of cultural performances and conversations. A number of the cultural festival's panels did focus on various interpretations of the book and included noted scholars and writers such as Thulani Davis, Sheila S. Walker, and Richard Long. Other panels, however, on topics such as "Afro Futurism" and "Post-Black Visual Arts," seemed to have at best a slim connection with *Souls*. The huge extravaganza was coordinated through the Fulton County, Georgia, Board of Commissioners and its Arts Council, but it was financed primarily by corporate America. Atlanta has become the South's capital for globalization, so it was only appropriate that both local and transnational corporations were on hand to celebrate Du Bois. A short list of prominent funders included Coca-Cola, Wachovia Bank, American Express, Lincoln Mercury, Delta Airlines, AT&T, Georgia Power, Turner Broadcasting Systems, and Altria Corporate Services. Once more, I was invited to give a lecture at the festival, this time on "The Politics of W. E. B. Du Bois and Global Consciousness." But it became clear after talking with one conference planner that no exhaustive critique of the text itself or the political context that had motivated Du Bois in the first place was desired.[4]

In New York City, several public events honoring *The Souls of Black Folk* were arranged. On April 7, historian Robin D. G. Kelley participated as a narrator during dramatic readings of excerpts from *Souls,* staged by author/playwright Thulani Davis. The dramatic readings, presented at the City University of New York Graduate School, also featured actors Danny Glover, Phylicia Rashad, and Jeffrey Wright. Funds for the event were donated by Trans-Africa, the premier black American lobby on behalf of African and Caribbean countries.[5] On October 17–18, 2003, the New York Historical Society sponsored a two-day symposium, *"The Souls of Black Folk in the Twenty-First Century,"* featuring a keynote address by Du Bois biographer David Levering Lewis. The conference's panel discussion on "the legacy of the book and its relevance to twenty-first century America" included prominent American historians Nell Painter, Eric Foner, and Patricia Sullivan.[6]

Harvard's highly esteemed African American studies program, named in honor of Du Bois, as expected, orchestrated a major event around *Souls*—a series of readings from the text held at Boston's Memorial Church on April 25, 2003. Celebrating "the centennial of the landmark work" were speakers Henry Louis Gates, Jr., Michael Dawson, Homi Bhabha, Anthony Appiah, Evelyn Brooks Higginbotham, and Du Bois's stepson, David Graham Du Bois. What was most significant about this event, however, was Gates's effort to reframe the meaning of both Du Bois and his book. "No one did more to place the American Negro in the world as a full-voiced speaking subject than did W. E. B. Du Bois," Gates noted in his opening remarks. Du Bois must be remembered for two principal contributions, Gates argued, "one political and one literary."[7] Du Bois's major political accomplishment was his role in creating the NAACP and being "one of the fathers of the Civil Rights Movement." His second major contribution was the invention of the literary "metaphors for the black condition" employed throughout *Souls,* which would be incorporated into the work of several generations of African American writers.

Gates was defining the quintessential Du Bois as a literary artist and liberal pragmatist, in effect cutting off from critical discussion the final forty years of Du Bois's public life.

The news media coverage and the public programs generated by the *Souls* centennial also emphasized a few key phrases or ideas expressed in the text. The most prominent was, of course, the most famous sentence Du Bois ever wrote in his long career—"the problem of the twentieth century is the problem of the color-line." "Du Bois could not have known when he wrote these words in 1903 that they'd remain an indelible part of the nation's discussions on race 100 years later," observed Anica Butler in the *Hartford Courant*. "Yet *The Souls of Black Folk*, Du Bois's influential, if not prescient, book of essays, has indeed endured and possibly has become even more relevant as an ever-shifting color line affects more than just black Americans."[8] *Washington Post* writer Lynne Duke led her story with Du Bois's famous quote, but not to praise it: "Excuse me, sir. I'm looking for the color line. Would you know where I can find it?" Duke claimed that Du Bois's formulation, while true enough a century ago, was an anachronism today. "Since Du Bois's day, the color line has gone undercover. No signs. No laws. No night riders in white sheets. And it's no longer a black-white thing," Duke added to distinguish the rigid racial context of the Jim Crow South from the multicultural, post–civil rights America of the twenty-first century. Duke's main point, that immigration and globalization have added "new shades of complexity to the color line," was fully anticipated by Du Bois and is actually central to his formulation of the problem.[9] The "color line" for Du Bois was never just black vs. white, but also "the relation of the darker to the lighter races of men in Asia and Africa, in America and the islands of the seas."

Du Bois's theory of double consciousness—that the African American was simultaneously "an American, a Negro; two souls, two thoughts, two unreconciled strivings"—garnered equal attention and commentary. Felicia Lee's *New York Times* article began with the double consciousness quotation, and described *Souls* as "both a depiction of black life in America and a meditation on the meaning of blackness."[10] Other frequently mentioned themes were Du Bois's bold advocacy of full civil rights and equality for blacks, his opposition to the conservative "accommodationism" of black educator Booker T. Washington, and his promulgation of the role of the "Talented Tenth"—college-educated, middle-class African Americans who were expected to lead the uplifting of the race. For *Nashville City*

Paper staff writer Ron Wynn, Du Bois was a "role model" who "felt that those blacks who are most gifted—he called them the 'talented tenth'—should not only receive the best training and preparation but also be equally willing to use their newly acquired skills to help others attain freedom." It was a shame, Wynn added, that "Du Bois became so disillusioned at his native land's treatment of African Americans that he renounced his U.S. citizenship" and died in Ghana.[11] Wynn's assertion was wrong on several counts. After Du Bois's indictment and subsequent legal vindication in federal court in 1951, his passport was nevertheless seized by the U.S. State Department, and it was withheld until 1958. The late Herbert Aptheker, Du Bois's literary executor, explained to me on several occasions that when Du Bois left the United States to travel to Ghana on October 5, 1961, it was with the expectation that he would eventually return to the United States. As David Levering Lewis also notes in his biography, "Du Bois became a citizen of Ghana" on his ninety-fifth birthday "largely because the American embassy refused to renew his passport."[12]

Much of the media focused on Du Bois's confrontation with black educator Booker T. Washington, the founder of the Tuskegee Institute and the most powerful African American political leader of the early 1900s. On Tavis Smiley's syndicated program on National Public Radio on April 17, 2003, two readers representing the views of Washington and Du Bois were alternated.[13] One widely reprinted United Press International column by Dallas journalist John Bloom grossly oversimplified the positions of both Washington and Du Bois, characterizing "Tuskegeeism" as "training up the black race in trades so they could be of economic value to the nation," with Du Bois holding "the opposite view." That explains, added Bloom, why African American college students at Du Bois's alma mater, Fisk University, "were more likely to be carrying French grammars and Latin-inscribed chapbooks than textbooks on agriculture."[14]

To their credit, many scholars made determined efforts to set the historical record straight, to explain the meaning of Du Bois's work without turning it into what journalist Lynne Duke described as an "almost sacred text."[15] Robin Kelley described Du Bois as "the most important American intellectual to reflect on the meaning of modernity in the Western world, with influence on all aspects of human science."[16] David Levering Lewis correctly characterized Du Bois's critique of Booker T. Washington as marking "the beginning of the modern civil rights movement," and in various publications cautioned against a narrow, elitist interpretation of what Du Bois meant by the

"Talented Tenth."[17] The most insightful appreciation of Du Bois and *Souls* to appear in the popular press was written by cultural studies scholar Stuart Hall in the (London) *Guardian*. Hall began his essay with the regret that Du Bois's "life and work are, alas, little known on this side of the Atlantic." Du Bois's lasting significance and relevance, Hall suggested, came from "his single-minded commitment to racial justice and his capacity to shape black consciousness." In *Souls,* culture and politics are inextricably linked, as part of the process of group self-awareness and affirmation. "Du Bois used language and ideas to hammer out a strategy for political equality," Hall observed, "and to sound the depths of the black experience in the aftermath of slavery." *The Souls of Black Folk,* for the first time in history, tried to paint for white America "a vivid portrait of black people in the decades after emancipation in 1862—how they lived and who they really were—and thus to enlighten white America—still profoundly attached to myths of black inferiority—as to the true meaning of being black in post–Civil War America."[18]

It is no exaggeration to say that *The Souls of Black Folk* has remained the most influential text about the African American experience for a century. Even Du Bois's contemporaries, whether agreeing with or dissenting from its various arguments, understood its unique power as a work of literature. James Weldon Johnson observed that *Souls* had "a greater effect upon and within the black race in America than any other single book published in this country since *Uncle Tom's Cabin.*"[19] A fuller appreciation of *The Souls of Black Folk* in our own time, more than a generation removed from the enactment of the Civil Rights Act of 1964, which outlawed legal racial segregation, requires a reconstruction of the context in which it was produced. The fourteen essays included in *Souls* were written between 1897 and 1903, the years Du Bois spent constructing his social science research projects at Atlanta University, in the heartland of an increasingly segregated and violent South. As Farah Jasmine Griffin has observed,

> Living in the American South—where his young son died of naso-pharyngeal diphtheria, having been denied the medical attention of white doctors; where the black farm worker Sam Hose was brutally lynched, burned, and mutilated in the same year; and where the Atlanta riots of 1906 destroyed a middle-class black community and killed both blacks and whites—Du Bois came to question the sufficiency of academic knowledge alone to address the problems facing those who lived within the veil.[20]

It was life in the South that eventually forced Du Bois to confront the human consequences of American structural racism, and its effects upon its most marginalized and vulnerable victims.

The details of Du Bois's life are of course well known, thanks in part to the deliberately semi-autobiographical character of many of his writings. He was born in Great Barrington, Massachusetts, on February 23, 1868, less than three years after the conclusion of the Civil War, and only five years after the Emancipation Proclamation. After his graduation from high school in Great Barrington, he was sent to Fisk University in Nashville, Tennessee. The experience at Fisk gave the young Du Bois his first real understanding of African American culture and life in the rural South. In *Souls,* Du Bois describes with loving attention his trials as a schoolteacher in rural Tennessee. Completing his bachelor's degree, Du Bois transferred to Harvard College, where he matriculated as a junior. In 1890 Du Bois was awarded his B.A. degree cum laude from Harvard. It was at his graduation ceremony that Du Bois first came to public attention. Selected as a commencement speaker, Du Bois provocatively selected as the subject of his oration "Jefferson Davis," the former president of the Confederacy. Du Bois's speech and his description of Davis as "the peculiar champion of a people fighting to be free in order that another people should not be free" were widely praised as fair.[21] The *Nation* noted with approval that the "slender, intellectual-looking mulatto" had "handled his difficult and hazardous subject with absolute good taste, great moderation and almost contemptuous fairness."[22]

Du Bois pursued his graduate studies at Harvard, and with the financial support of a scholarship from the Slater Fund, he attended the University of Berlin and traveled extensively throughout Europe from 1892 to 1894. Du Bois was awarded the Ph.D. in history from Harvard in 1895 and his dissertation, "The Suppression of the African Slave-Trade to the United States of America, 1638–1870," was published the following year as the initial volume in the Harvard Historical Studies Series. Although Du Bois was the first African American to receive a Ph.D. from Harvard University, he was not offered employment at any white academic institution. He taught briefly at Wilberforce University, a historically black college in Ohio, and from 1896 to 1897 was employed by the University of Pennsylvania to conduct a social survey of Philadelphia's black community. The study that was produced from this project, *The Philadelphia Negro,* represented the first social science examination of race and racism in an urban context. In 1897, Du Bois received an appointment as a professor of history and economics at Atlanta University, where he immediately launched an ambitious series of annual research conferences dedicated to the study of the American Negro.

Du Bois's scholarly productivity during these years was remarkable, especially considering his extensive involvement in civic activities, international efforts to build a pan-Africanist movement, and his frequent forays into public debates as a journalist. Working with Trinidadian barrister Henry Sylvester Williams, Du Bois helped organize the first Pan-African Conference in London in August 1900, initiating a transnational process that a half century later would culminate in powerful independence movements across Africa and the Caribbean. In 1897, Du Bois along with noted scholar Alexander Crummell and other black intellectuals established the American Negro Academy, the first black academic society in the United States. The objective of the American Negro Academy—to encourage a cultural and intellectual renaissance among blacks in America—in many ways anticipated the Harlem Renaissance of the 1920s and the Negritude movement that followed. What must be kept in mind is that all these wide-ranging intellectual endeavors occurred at a time of extreme political repression for African Americans, especially in the U.S. South. Several hundred blacks were being lynched annually in the region throughout the 1890s. In 1896, the U.S. Supreme Court, in its *Plessy v. Ferguson* decision, established the legality of the "separate but equal" standard, which justified racial segregation in public accommodations, schools, and nearly all other aspects of public life. In 1890, Mississippi took the lead in disfranchising its black electorate, and other southern states soon followed. By the early 1900s, local ordinances had been adopted that for all practical purposes created parallel racial universes separating black and white Americans. Blacks could not run for elective office and in most cases were denied the right to vote; they were not permitted to attend whites-only schools, or to patronize whites-only restrooms, restaurants, and hotels. Blacks would soon be excluded from juries, denied admission to theatres and other public amusements except in racially segregated seating sections, and refused access to many hospitals.

It was against this brutal background of white supremacy and black subordination that Booker T. Washington emerged as a national spokesman on issues of race. In 1881, Washington had established the Tuskegee Institute in Alabama, which by 1900 was the largest postsecondary school for Negroes in the world. In September 1895, Washington catapulted to national attention by delivering a short address at the Cotton States and International Exposition in Atlanta; this speech would later be described as the "Atlanta Compromise." In effect, Washington appeared to surrender any overt claim to voting and equal rights for African Americans. He appeared to accept the reality of racial segregation, declaring that "in all things that are purely social we can be as separate as the fingers, yet one as the hand in all things essential to mutual progress."[23] In return African Americans would expect opportunities for landownership, business development, and vocational training in the South. Washington urged blacks to build their own institutions, creating and distributing goods and services for black consumers, utilizing racial segregation as a buffer to sustain a separate economy. Washington's pragmatic approach to segregation appealed to many African American small-business owners, farmers, and educators in industrial training schools.

For decades in black American political culture, the legend of the powerful ideological struggle between Booker T. Washington and W. E. B. Du Bois has grown and hardened into virtual inevitability. In truth, Du Bois was not that far apart from the "Wizard of Tuskegee"—as Washington was occasionally described by his supporters. Days after Washington delivered the Atlanta Compromise address, Du Bois sent him a glowing note of congratulations for his "phenomenal success in Atlanta—it was a word fitly spoken."[24] Du Bois worried about criticisms of Washington that soon appeared in the African American press, and he promptly forwarded a letter to the *New York Age* in the Tuskegeean's defense. Washington's controversial proposal, Du Bois believed, "might be the basis of a real settlement between whites and blacks in the South, if the South opened to the Negroes the doors of economic opportunity and the Negroes co-operated with the South in political sympathy."[25]

Washington reciprocated these gestures of friendship and esteem from Du Bois. In early 1900, the position of superintendent of Washington, D.C.'s Negro schools was advertised, and although Du Bois did not actively seek the appointment, Washington pushed for him. In a letter dated March 11, 1900, Washington informed the black scholar that he had "recommended" him "as strongly as I could."[26] In the summer of 1901, Du Bois and his family were invited to be house guests at Washington's West Virginia residence. In July 1902, Washington praised Du Bois's scholarship on the state of black public schools in the South.[27] In his 1944 essay, "My Evolving Program for Negro Freedom," Du Bois also made it clear that he "was not overcritical of Booker T. Washington" during these years. Du Bois wrote that in 1902 he met with Washington privately to discuss the possibility of leaving Atlanta University and transferring his various research projects to Tuskegee Institute. "If I had been offered a chance at Tuskegee to pursue my program of investigation, with larger funds and opportunity, I would doubtless have accepted," Du Bois admitted, "because by that time, despite my liking for Atlanta, I saw that the university would not long be able to finance my work."[28] Most of the militant black intellectuals and political activists who had taken public positions against Washington's policies of accommodation, such as Boston *Guardian* editor William Monroe Trotter and crusading antilynching journalist Ida B. Wells-Barnett, did not consider Du Bois a "radical." In July 1902, for example, Trotter was complaining to his friends that Du Bois was not to be trusted or relied on in the struggle against Washington.[29]

Ideologically and even in terms of public policy, Du Bois and Washington were again not far apart. Washington emphasized the importance of practical vocational training for Negroes, 90 percent of whom lived in rural areas and mostly worked in agriculture. Du Bois viewed colleges and industrial schools as being complementary, and always acknowledged the significant role of trade schools and vocational training. In the late 1890s, for example, Du Bois had proposed a plan of cooperation between the research conferences then being held regularly at Hampton Institute and Atlanta University. In 1901, Du Bois publicly applauded the Tuskegee Institute's decade-long campaign against the worst effects of the sharecropping system on the black community. On the issue of black business development, both men were largely in accord. Du Bois strongly favored black entrepreneurship as a sign of the race's growing capacity to do for itself. In his 1898 speech, on the "Meaning of Business," Du Bois preached that African Americans had to accumulate capital and invest it constructively. "The day the Negro race courts and marries the savings-bank," Du Bois predicted, "will be the day of its salvation."[30] Washington was for all practical purposes the "father of black capitalism"—founder of the National Negro Business League, proponent of black entrepreneurship, and advocate of black property ownership. Based on the historical evidence, then, it is a mistake to read backward across time to judge the Washington–Du Bois conflict as inevitable.

In 1902 a small publishing house in Chicago, A.C. McClurg and Company, contacted Du Bois to inquire if he had any material that could be published as a book. Du Bois's first choice would have been to produce "a social study which should be perhaps a summing up of the work of the Atlanta Conferences, or at any rate, a scientific investigation," he wrote later in *Dusk of Dawn*. But McClurg suggested a different kind of book, a volume of collected essays that for the most part had been previously published. "I demurred," Du Bois later wrote, "because books of essays almost always fall so flat. Nevertheless, I got together a number of my fugitive pieces."[31] Although the essays he selected for *Souls* had been written over a period of seven years, designed originally for very different audiences and covering a broad range of topics, they nevertheless had many things in common. As Farah Jasmine Griffin has observed, one central element was "Du Bois's consistent use of the first person, his insertion of himself as a subjective student and participant in black life and culture." In several previously published essays, Du Bois had already developed the effective concept of the "veil" metaphor to represent the structural barriers between the black and white segregated worlds. His repeated references to the concept helped bring a thematic coherence to the new work as a whole. As Griffin notes, in most of the essays "Du Bois turns to academic fields of knowledge such as history, sociology, and philosophy to assist in his interpretation of the complexity of black lives. While these fields help to provide the framework for his analysis, his prose is shaped by biblical and mythological narrative, metaphor and allusion."[32]

What is most striking to me about *Souls* as a political statement is the *moderation* of its tone. If Du Bois had not written "Of Mr. Booker T. Washington and Others," *Souls* would have been still essentially the same book in its contents, but would probably not have been perceived as a radical challenge to Jim Crow. In his essay "Of the Sons of Master and Man," for instance, Du Bois carefully draws out the logical reasons why most southern whites feared the extension of equal rights to African Americans. In language that was remarkably similar to Washington's, Du Bois called upon southern whites and blacks alike to set aside their prejudices—"to see and appreciate and sympathize with each other's position, for the Negro to realize more deeply than he does at present the need of uplifting the masses of his people, for white people to realize more vividly than they have yet done the deadening and disastrous effect of ... color prejudice."

Interracial progress is possible, Du Bois suggested, "only by a union of intelligence and sympathy across the color-line."

As the book manuscript was being prepared for shipment to the publisher, either in late 1902 or early 1903, Du Bois made the final decision to insert "Of Booker T. Washington and Others." Why? Nearly forty years later, Du Bois explained that he was "increasingly uncomfortable under the statements of Mr. Washington's position: his depreciation of the value of the vote; his evident dislike of Negro colleges; and his general attitude which seemed to place the onus of the blame for the status of Negroes upon the Negroes themselves rather than upon the whites."[33] Yet we now know, from the private correspondence of both men and from other evidence, that they continued to cooperate with each other at this time. Washington privately offered his assistance to Du Bois, for example, in pursuing legal action against the Pullman Company for racial discrimination. Only several months prior to the publication of *Souls,* Washington and Du Bois came together publicly to denounce the exclusion of blacks from consideration as candidates for Rhodes scholarships in the Atlanta area.[34] In early May 1903, just as the newly printed *Souls* was being shipped to bookstores in the South, Du Bois was preparing to teach summer school at Tuskegee Institute, where he was living on campus. I strongly suspect that Du Bois did not anticipate that his measured words of what he considered constructive criticism would be universally interpreted as a complete rupture from Tuskegee. Even in his essay, Du Bois characterized Washington as "certainly the most distinguished Southerner since Jefferson Davis, and the one with the largest personal following." The essay called upon "the black men of America" to oppose only "part of the work of their greatest leader. So far as Mr. Washington preaches Thrift, Patience, and Industrial Training for the Masses, we must hold up his hands and strive with him.... But so far as Mr. Washington apologizes for injustice North or South, does not rightly value the privilege and duty of voting, belittles the emasculating effects of caste distinctions ... we must unceasingly and firmly oppose them."[35]

Nothing Du Bois had previously written prepared him for the avalanche of public reaction generated by *The Souls of Black Folk.* One of the earliest reviews appeared in the April 18, 1903, issue of Trotter's *Guardian,* entitled *"Souls of Black Folk:* A Great Book by a Great Scholar, Touching the Spiritual Life of Colored People." The *Guardian* praised Du Bois for writing "with the eloquence of a poet, with the foresight of a prophet, with the vigor of a reformer, and with the power only he can possess who has thought deeply upon the wrongs of his own people." The *Guardian* review emphasized Du Bois's critique of Washington: "In his consideration of that modern movement of which Mr. Booker T. Washington is the leader, Mr. Du Bois speaks strongly of the man who he believes is striving for much and accomplishing but little."[36] Within days of the *Guardian*'s glowing tribute to *Souls,* there appeared a sharply negative and boldly racist review in the *New York Times.* "It is generally conceded that Booker T. Washington represents the best hope of the negro in America," the review began. Du Bois clearly "does not understand his own people in their natural state as does [Washington].... Yet it is equally certain that 'The Souls of Black Folk' throws much light upon the complexities of the negro problem, for it shows that the keynote of at least some negro aspiration is still the abolition of the social color-line. For it is the Jim Crow car, and the fact that he may not smoke a cigar and drink a cup of tea with a white man in the South, that most galls William E. Burghardt Du Bois of the Atlanta College for Negroes."[37] Equally brutal was a review in the *Colored American,* a newspaper closely aligned with Washington. It accused Du Bois of being simply a "hanger-on at a place created by white people"; the author's inclusion of the essay critical of Washington in his volume was an opportunistic publicity stunt, because *The Souls of Black Folk* would have found few readers on "its own bottom." The *Colored American* urged the president of Atlanta University, Horace Bumstead, to curb "the outgivings and ill-advised criticism of the learned Doctor who is now in his employ."[38]

A number of the early reviews followed the lead of the *New York Times* and roundly condemned Du Bois, focusing primarily on two issues—his criticisms of Washington and his opposition to racial segregation and disenfranchisement. The *Outlook*'s May 23, 1903, issue misinterpreted Du Bois's double-consciousness theory as meaning that "the negro and the American are ever separate, though in the same personality.... The sense of amused contempt and pity for his own race, caught from the white people, is reflected in the title of Professor Du Bois's book, 'The Souls of the Black Folk.'" The differences between Du Bois and Washington reflected two divergent "influences in the negro race.... One of these parties is ashamed of the race, the other is proud of it ... one wishes to teach the negro to read the Ten Commandments in Hebrew, the other wishes first to teach him to obey them in English."[39] The review of *Souls* appearing in the July

1903 issue of the *South Atlantic Quarterly* correctly interpreted the "veil" metaphor, but then praised Washington for embracing racial segregation and for "glorify[ing] the negro race until it shall be no dishonor to be black. Du Bois would chafe and fret, and tear his heart out. And as for us, who are a divinely appointed superior race, how much do we do to render the burden lighter to either the one or the other?" The reviewer, John Spencer Basset, who edited the *South Atlantic Quarterly*, acknowledged that "Du Bois's protest is not a violent one. It is a cry of a man who suffers.... (I)t bears the evidence that its author while he was writing realized the hopelessness of it all."[40] The *American Monthly Review of Reviews* suggested that *Souls* "deserves a wide reading," but not for the accuracy of its views. "Professor Du Bois is a man of the highest culture, and he cannot overcome the sensitiveness natural to a man of fine feelings placed in the position he occupies.... The result is truly pathetic."[41]

Other reviews were less critical, but the reviewers were so completely overwhelmed by their racism that they were unable to comprehend or interpret the meaning of *Souls*. A typical example is represented by the review of Theophilus Bolden Steward in the July 1903 issue of the *American Journal of Sociology.* "Professor Du Bois approaches the many-sided negro question with the confidence and conviction of a master, and with the grace and beauty of a poet," Steward noted. "The author is at his best in an unbiased consideration of the negro's emotional nature.... There can be no doubt that the preponderance of misdirected emotionalism is evidenced in the rapidity with which the negro swings from love to hate, from laughter to tears." Steward applauded Du Bois's discussion of the inequalities affecting rural African Americans in the South's "Black Belt," and praised the chapters "Of the Faith of the Fathers" and "The Sorrow Songs" as vividly depicting "the credulity of the negro and the power of his soul to express in plaintive melody his soul-sorrows and strivings." Yet on balance, Steward reflected, *Souls* offered no "practical solution of the color-line problem ... Professor Du Bois's book cannot be said to do more than offer rich hints from a vast store of sympathy and knowledge."[42]

Despite these negative reviews, public demand for *Souls* was strong, and A.C. McClurg and Company subsequently ordered a second, and soon a third, printing. As the book circulated nationally, it attracted reviews from more liberal publications, which immediately recognized the significance of Du Bois's accomplishment. The *Nation*'s June 11, 1903, issue announced that "Du Bois has written a profoundly interesting and affecting book, remarkable as a piece of literature apart from its inner significance." Most surprising to the *Nation* was the power of the author's passion reflected throughout the text. Those "who have heard Mr. Du Bois speak" and found him "coldly intellectual, have not been at all prepared for the emotion and the passion throbbing here in every chapter, almost every page. It is almost intolerably sad."[43] The *Congregationalist and Christian World* applauded *Souls* as "almost the first fully articulate voice from what the author calls 'the veil'—the full expression of the soul of a people. It does not matter that Professor Du Bois is Massachusetts born; long years of work among his fellow Negroes in the South have given him a right to speak for the children of the slaves in their difficult effort to make real a race aspiration in the face of a higher and hostile environment." This reviewer also agreed with Du Bois's balanced criticisms of Washington, adding, "We are not ready to admit that the higher education of the Negro has been a failure."[44] The New York *Independent* observed that Du Bois's book "makes plain" the "pitiful injustice—industrial, political, and social—meted out to the negro by his lords and masters of the Anglo-Saxon race in America."[45] The Los Angeles publication *Outwest* praised *Souls* as an "eloquent and penetrating discussion" of American race relations. "The voice of a man, lifted to tell unstutteringly those truths concerning life which burn hottest in his own heart, is always worth an attentive ear. And if the voice be both trained and melodious, its utterances are, in the finest sense, Literature. *The Souls of Black Folk* falls, without possibility of dispute, under this category."[46]

By the summer of 1903, a number of articles that may have been originally assigned to review *The Souls of Black Folk* pretty much ignored the contents of the book and speculated about the growing ideological controversy between Washington and Du Bois. The (London) *Times Literary Supplement* of August 14, 1903, described *Souls* as "an extraordinary compound of emotion and statistics, of passionate revolt and sober restraint." But the real question worth pursuing, the reviewer suggested, was what *Souls* represented in regard to the future of black leadership in America. "There are, it seems, two schools of thought among educated Negroes; the one, led by Mr. Booker Washington, would abandon the struggle for political power and higher education and pursue the conciliation of the South and the acquisition of wealth; the other, headed by the present author, would break down the color prejudice by higher education and civil rights." This reviewer then made what was, in retrospect, a remarkable prediction: "If there should ever arise a leader of the caliber of Professor Du Bois who could command the allegiance of all educated negroes, events more dramatic than the gradual decay of color-prejudice might come to pass."[47]

How did Du Bois respond to this sudden explosion of interest in his work, and both the praises and bitter criticisms *Souls* had provoked? One excellent insight is provided by a lengthy interview with the author that appeared in the June 16, 1903, *Chicago Daily Tribune* under the headline "Cultured Negro Model for Race." The *Tribune* reporter, "Raymond," described an evening spent with Du Bois, depicting the scene at Atlanta University in vivid detail: "After trudging up two flights of stairs, through bare, uncarpeted halls, one suddenly finds himself transported into the busy literary workshop of a close student. Seated at the center of a big table, revolving easily in his office chair, alert, intelligent, conservative, weighing his words cautiously, and yet speaking with the confidence born of profound study, the picture of this brown-skinned, well-dressed, self-poised scholar was not soon to be forgotten." Du Bois expressed surprise at the public attention focusing on *Souls,* the *Tribune* reporter explained, "because he was the author of many other works which he believes more important." The interview focused largely on Du Bois's general views about the state of race relations, the benefits of higher education for Negroes, and the link between political and economic power. Du Bois did not directly mention Washington, but the reporter could not avoid the obvious differences between the two men. "Professor Du Bois believes that the salvation of his race must come through the exercise of the right of franchise as the necessary preliminary to commercial equality," the *Tribune* reporter concluded. "The line of cleavage between this element of Negroes and that represented by Booker T. Washington is daily becoming more marked, and this is a pity, because two such men as Du Bois and Washington, undoubtedly the brainiest of their race, ought to be brought together to work more in harmony for the ultimate uplifting of their own people."[48]

In early May 1903, a forum to discuss *Souls* was held in Chicago. It included Tuskegee Institute Professor Monroe Work, journalist Ida B. Wells-Barnett, and her husband Ferdinand Barnett, the first African American assistant state's attorney in Illinois. On May 30, Wells-Barnett wrote to Du Bois about the forum, observing that "we are still reading your book with the same delighted appreciation."[49] Novelist Charles Chesnutt suggested to Du Bois that *The Souls of*

Black Folk might have had some "direct effect in stirring up the peonage investigation" then taking place in Alabama.[50] From the British West African colony of the Gold Coast, attorney and author Casely Hayford sent a letter of congratulations to Du Bois: "I have recently had the pleasure of reading your great work, 'The Souls of Black Folk,' and it occurred to me if leading thinkers of the African race in America had the opportunity of exchanging thoughts with the thinkers of the African race in West Africa, this century would be likely to see the race problem solved."[51] Prominent German social scientist Max Weber contacted Du Bois, insisting that his "splendid work ... ought *to be translated into German.*" [Weber's emphasis] Weber proposed a suitable translator for the task, and then offered "to write a short introduction about the Negro question and literature and should be much obligated to you for some information about your life, viz: age, birthplace, descent, positions held by you—of course only *if you give* your authorization."[52] And from Ithaca, New York, a young black woman in her junior year of undergraduate studies at Cornell University, Jessie Fauset, sent to Du Bois on December 26, 1903, a letter of appreciation for *Souls*: "I am glad, glad you wrote it—we have needed someone to voice the intricacies of the blind maze of thought and action along which the modern, educated colored man or woman struggles. It hurt you to write that book, didn't it? The man of fine sensibilities has to suffer exquisitely, just simply because his feeling is so fine."[53]

It would take a year or more for Du Bois to fully appreciate what *The Souls of Black Folk* had set into motion. In a revealing short essay in the *Independent,* published in November 1904, Du Bois reflected critically about the work and the unexpected storm of controversy it had created. *Souls* "is a series of fourteen essays written under various circumstances and for different purposes," Du Bois noted. "It has, therefore, considerable, perhaps too great, diversity.... All this leads to rather abrupt transitions of style, tone and viewpoint and, too, without doubt, to a distinct sense of incompleteness and sketchiness." Nevertheless, *Souls* retained "a unity of purpose." Du Bois explained that he had deliberately employed throughout the text "a personal and intimate tone of self-revelation. In each essay I sought to speak from within—to depict a world as we see it who dwell therein." Then in a remarkable passage that seemingly repudiated the double-consciousness theory, Du Bois mused: "In its larger aspects the style is tropical—African. This needs no apology. The blood of my fathers spoke through me and cast off the English restraint of my training and surroundings. The resulting accomplishment is a matter of taste. Sometimes I think very well of it and sometimes I do not."[54]

Few books make history, and fewer still become foundational texts for the movements and struggles of an entire people. *The Souls of Black Folk* occupies this rare position. It helped to create the intellectual argument for the black freedom struggle in the twentieth century; it justified the pursuit of higher education for Negroes and thus contributed to the rise of the black middle class; it described a global color line, and therefore anticipated Pan-Africanism and colonial revolutions in the Third World; its stunning critique of how "race" is lived through the normal aspects of daily life is central to what would become known as "whiteness studies" a century later. The best way to fully appreciate the lasting message and meaning of *Souls* is to place it within a broader study of the extraordinary person who produced it—Du Bois.

Souls marked the real beginning of Du Bois's incomparable career as a scholar-activist, a career that ended on the shores of West Africa. Although Du Bois's personal politics changed over these years, the popularity and prominence of *The Souls of Black Folk* in many ways continued to define him in the public imagination. Consequently, Du Bois was extremely pleased that successive generations of young people encountering black history and literature for the first time were frequently introduced to his legendary collection of essays as their basic primer. As Du Bois's views came increasingly under fire during the Cold War, he became concerned that *Souls* might go out of print. In January 1949, he purchased the printing plates and rights to *Souls* from the publisher for one hundred dollars. Du Bois asked a young Marxist historian and friend, Herbert Aptheker, for his advice about "what can be done with them." Du Bois's initial thought was to undertake "possibly a sort of jubilee edition," and he asked Aptheker to contact novelist Howard Fast for his advice.[55] A well-known writer and member of the Communist Party, Fast was also a close friend of the writer Shirley Graham, whom Du Bois married in 1951. Fast's most famous novel, *Freedom Road,* a fictionalized interpretation of Reconstruction, had drawn heavily on Du Bois's classic study *Black Reconstruction.* Fast had established the Blue Heron Press, a publishing house designed to feature his own writings as well as the works of communist intellectuals who had been forced underground by the repression of McCarthyism. The necessary funds were raised for Blue Heron Press to produce the fiftieth-anniversary edition of *The Souls of Black Folk* sometime in 1953.[56]

As plans progressed for the jubilee reprinting of *Souls,* Du Bois began having second thoughts about his book. During a lecture tour of the West Coast in February 1953, a friend gave Du Bois a copy of *The Souls of Black Folk.* "I have had a chance to read it in part for the first time in years," Du Bois confided to Aptheker. In chapters seven, eight, and nine, Du Bois was deeply troubled to find five negative "incidental references to Jews.... As I re-read these words today, I see that harm might come if they were allowed to stand as they are." Du Bois now questioned whether "the foreign exploiters, to whom I referred in my study of the Black Belt, were in fact Jews." But even if some of the exploiting merchants Du Bois had described happened to be Jewish, he had not recognized "that by stressing the name of the group instead of what some members of the [group] may have done, I was unjustly maligning a people in the exact same way my folk were then and are now falsely accused."[57] Over the next few months Du Bois changed his mind several times about what would be most appropriate—leaving the original text as it was or revising the book. By the summer of 1953, according to Aptheker, Du Bois had made revisions at seven places for the 1953 edition. In the new foreword, Du Bois mentioned that certain changes had been made in the text, "but did not otherwise identify them or comment upon them."[58] Du Bois also inserted into the new introduction his belief that *Souls* did not adequately anticipate the significance of the rise of psychoanalytic theory and had failed to recognize the fundamental role of class in shaping the contours of society. The Blue Heron edition came off the press in October 1953.

It is a striking measure of Du Bois's status as a political "nonperson" in the United States in the final decade of his life that much of his scholarly and polemical writing from this time is still unavailable. Du Bois's large manuscript, "Russia and America," containing his reflections on the evolution of the Soviet Union, was rejected for publication by Harcourt, Brace and Company, and remains unpublished. His third and final summation of his life's journey, *The Autobiography of W. E. B. Du Bois,* was printed in the Soviet Union in Russian six years before an English-language edition was released in the United States. His small monograph, *Africa: Toward a History of the Continent,* was printed in Russian but, according to Du Bois biographer David Levering Lewis, "remains unavailable in English."[59] In the rush to celebrate *The Souls of Black Folk* in 2003, few of the programs reflected critically on the complex politics of the book's history, the Blue Heron edition of 1953, and the continuing suppression of part of Du Bois's intellectual and political legacy. It is indeed a curious historical paradox that the organization that once fired Du Bois and which coldly withdrew its support when he was falsely prosecuted by the U.S. government as a Soviet agent now raises millions of dollars from corporate America to celebrate his leonine image and the wrong edition of his most famous book. Du Bois's leadership and writings largely gave birth to the Talented Tenth, but as a group they lack his courage and vision. Not until Du Bois's entire intellectual history and political evolution are critically studied and understood will African Americans and others comprehend what the "new color line" means in today's context of globalization. Because indeed, the problem of the twenty-first century is the problem of global apartheid—the unequal distribution of wealth, resources, and power and the disproportionate poverty, poor health, and hunger that divide the affluent north from the oppressed south transnationally across the world.

No single individual was more influential in constructing modern black America and in articulating a theory of human equality that successfully culminated in the partial reconstruction of American democracy than William Edward Burghardt Du Bois. *Souls* is the best starting point for understanding the man and his times. The common denominator in Du Bois's thinking throughout his magnificent sojourn was his fierce pursuit of justice, particularly for people of African descent. As Dr. Martin Luther King, Jr., observed in February 1968, only weeks before his assassination, "Dr. Du Bois's greatest virtue was his committed empathy with all the oppressed and his divine dissatisfaction with all forms of injustice."[60]

2

Searching for the Souls of Black Women

W. E. B. Du Bois's Contribution

Elizabeth Higginbotham

Seeing Black women and appreciating their social location have been a challenge for many scholars. W. E. B. Du Bois's contributions to understanding Black women are significant. He was a keen observer of social life and placed those findings in a context of national and international systems. As Cheryl Townsend Gilkes wrote, "His cultural autobiography was shaped by his conscious observations of women's lives. As a result, his work is the earliest self-consciously sociological interpretation of the role of African American women as agents of social change."[1]

It is difficult to see and study Black women in this nation. The U.S. Census did not even differentiate Negro persons by sex until 1830.[2] In Du Bois's words, Black women were excluded from the "worship of women"; that status was reserved for certain majority group women.[3] Yet in sociology, as in many fields, it has been hard to grasp the complexities that shape Black women's lives when there is little regard for the class and racial foundations that enable a group to "expect" a particular cluster of behaviors from its men or its women. It is important to look at Du Bois's work and how his thinking could inform our understanding of Black women's lives over the past century. My comments are based on a reading of Du Bois's *The American Negro Family* and other works.[4] *The American Negro Family* includes social studies made by college students of contemporary homes, family composition and lifestyles, and earnings, as well as reports from the annual conference for the Study of Negro Problems held at Atlanta University in 1908.

The American Negro Family is an important part of the legacy of social research at Atlanta University, where students and scholars collected and then integrated data with existing scholarship to challenge contemporary stereotypes about Black people.[5] Data on the conditions faced by the Negro family informed discussions within the Black community about the nature and magnitude of social problems and provided fuel for the quest for political and social rights. Although Du Bois's book provides evidence of the contributions Black women made to the family, it does not speak to the larger issue of how to frame Black women's social location.

The American Negro Family includes sections on Africa under the topics of marriage, the home, and the family economy. Du Bois did not argue that "Negro Americans are Africans," but he acknowledged that "there is a distinct nexus between Africa and America which, though broken and perverted, is nevertheless not to be neglected by the careful student."[6] The volume also has data on the West Indies, acknowledging the diaspora and the direct impact of different conditions of slavery and freedom on the Black family. Although there is great unevenness in the data—some information refers to individual cities or counties—when possible, comparisons between the years 1890 and 1900 chart the progress of the race and the nature of its problems. For example, we can see the beginnings of White flight, how racism and sexism in labor markets shaped very different lives for men and women in cities and rural communities early in the twentieth century, and the survival patterns families employed in both settings.

In *The American Negro Family,* Du Bois was forging weapons to wage a battle against the scientific racism of his era. By organizing empirical data and introducing new theoretical frameworks that draw on anthropology and small cultural studies, Du Bois attempted to place the Negro experience within a sociological perspective and to challenge the thinking that the Negro problem was about "natural inferiority." Family portraits in the book provide an early record of the values and activities of the Black folks who were not poor. Du Bois challenged common assumptions of Black inferiority and supported the argument that identifies sources of social conditions outside of biology. Du Bois's quest was a significant one, and he had few fellow travelers because most educated thinkers were wedded to notions of race being linked to abilities.

Scientific racism justified the racial divide between Negroes and White people. Most of the scholars in the early twentieth century did not even think in terms of injustice or employment discrimination.[7] The assumed inferiority of Black folks justified their exclusion from many institutions, such as industrial jobs and educational settings as well as their continued disenfranchisement in the South. Scientific racism was not just about Black folks. Immigrants from eastern and southern Europe were racialized, too, and their immigration was regulated with low quotas by the Johnson-Reed Act of 1924. This legislation also closed our nation as much as possible to Asian immigrants. Thinking about race in terms of biology, Theodore Roosevelt predicted the "suicide of the American race of Anglo-Saxons as it was overrun by emigrant mongrels."[8] What passed for research at that time supported an immigration policy that sought to keep the nation White as it was defined at that time. We are still wrestling with that complex legacy.

Gilkes noted that the exclusion of Du Bois from the developing field of sociology had implications for the way that people talked about race as well as gender and cultural theory. If Du Bois's work, particularly *The Souls of Black Folk*, had been taken seriously as sociology, according to Gilkes, we would have had more opportunities to "ask and answer questions from within the veil," and perhaps there would have been earlier use of multiple methodologies incorporating biographical, historical, and cultural materials.[9] In particular, we might have granted more agency to Black women. Instead, our field, influenced by biased histories, promoted poor sociology, particularly when it turned its attention to Black women. In the words of Patricia Morton, Black women were seen "as the linchpin of Negro pathology and cultural inferiority."[10] We can argue the degree to which distortions still exist, but some of the issues that Du Bois saw would clearly reshape the lens employed to view the experiences of Black women in the United States.

This discussion of Du Bois's contribution to the search for Black women's souls is limited to material from *The American Negro Family* as well as *The Souls of Black Folk* and "The Damnation of Women," a 1920 essay that appeared in *Darkwater: Voices from within the Veil*.[11] My comments are also informed by other feminists who have examined Du Bois's work, particularly Gilkes, Patricia Hill

Collins, and Farah Jasmine Griffin.[12] As I write these comments, I am cognizant of the critiques many feminists have made of Du Bois. I think it is important to understand the times in which Du Bois lived rather than hold him to more contemporary standards for viewing race and gender. My objective here is to follow Gilkes's idea to look at this important American sociologist and his relationship to American sociology.[13] What could sociologists learn from Du Bois's work? In particular, how could they improve the perspective for understanding the experiences of Black women?

I explore three major themes presented in Du Bois's early work that can help us understand the unique social location of Black women. The themes are the suffering of Black women, Black women's work as a path to economic independence, and the complexities of Black women's roles in preserving family and community. If mainstream scholars had wrestled with these ideas in Du Bois's time, the field of sociology might have had more debates about the sources of social behavior, and we might have had fewer distorted images of Black women. Before launching into my arguments, I want to make it clear that these issues are "all part of an intersectional paradigm" because, as Collins reminds us, they reflect how Du Bois saw race, class, and nation not as "personal identity categories, but as social hierarchies that shaped African Americans' access to status, property, and power."[14] Working and living behind the veil, Du Bois understood the enormity of oppression and some of what it meant for women.

First, Du Bois was keenly aware of the suffering of Black women. It is hard to think and write about suffering and pain, much less factor them into our statistical equations. It is not just the acute or chronic pain of physical discomfort that can drive one to distraction or inactivity. Instead, Du Bois saw "black women's suffering as a social fact that provides an important and distinct angle of vision."[15] Grounded in issues of rights, this suffering is part of the work experience and is key to women's relationships to the family and the wider community. In "The Damnation of Women," Du Bois wrote, "The crushing weight of slavery fell on black women. Under it there was no legal marriage, no legal family, and no legal control over children."[16] Only recently have scholars begun to investigate how gender shaped the American experience of slavery.[17] The reality of being a beast of burden that comes with enslavement is coupled with sexual exploitation for women as "they were forced to work, and in addition, they were forced to have sexual intercourse, bear children, and often nurse the children of others with their own bodies."[18]

Such a reality was not episodic but a historical and social fact that shaped people's sense of themselves and their world. One of the most famous escapes from slavery, the train ride to freedom of Ellen and William Craft, illustrates this point. Ellen, being light in color, posed as a White man with an injury so that she would not have to talk during the trip, while William accompanied her as a servant. The trip involved some tense moments, but they successfully traveled to Philadelphia. The Crafts delayed having children until they escaped to freedom because, as William presents in their narrative, "My wife was torn from her mother's embrace in childhood, and taken to a distant part of the country. She had seen so many other children separated from their parents in this cruel manner that the mere thought of her ever becoming a mother under the wretched system of American slavery appeared to fill her very soul with horror."[19] "No legal marriage, no legal family, and no legal control over children"[20] is a setup for suffering. People can shape such an institution only if they see others as less than human. So out of that American brand of slavery, we have the images that accompany it, whereby Black women were denied the acknowledgment of their suffering because they were assumed to be naturally base and immoral and to possess other negative characteristics designed to excuse the oppressor for unjust acts.[21]

Du Bois further stated in "The Damnation of Women" that he would never forgive the White South for "its wanton and continued and persistent insulting of the black womanhood which it sought and seeks to prostitute to its lust."[22] Du Bois took this "history of insult and degradation" seriously in terms of how Black people resisted as well as the ideological justifications for mistreatment that informed how many White Americans viewed Black women and supported denying them rights and dignities. In addition to their enduring both economic and political exploitation, Collins identified how negative stereotypes or controlling images of African American women justify their oppression. "Within U.S. culture, racist and sexist ideologies permeate the social structure to such a degree that they become hegemonic, namely, seen as natural, normal and inevitable."[23] During Du Bois's era, Black women were discussed by powerful White people, including many scholars, in negative terms. Furthermore, they were represented in the media and material culture in ways that emphasized either their low status or their willingness to serve others.[24] Ideology constitutes an additional dimension in the web of oppression that Black women face. Black Americans, along with other oppressed groups who are maligned in the media, have to combat such images that devalue them and further complicate their struggles for legal and civil rights.

A lack of power and legal protections shaped critical aspects of Black women's lives. The nexus continued to be a source of pain and suffering, yet the larger society did not fully appreciate their pain because controlling images suggested that they do not suffer. This practice is not the dissemblance described by Darlene Clark Hine, that is, establishing distance from suffering to protect the self.[25] Instead, this misrepresentation suggests a cultural reluctance to acknowledge Black women's suffering. Black women have had to struggle to give their experiences meaning in the historical moment. Yet, now some revisions of that history seek to assuage either guilt or shame. These efforts might reflect a need to alter some painful pictures, but the misrepresentations depict Black women in questionable ways. For example, the CBS television movie *Sally Hemmings: An American Scandal* shows the enslaved Hemmings as the initiator of her sexual relationship with Thomas Jefferson. The screenplay is fictional because it represents Hemmings as having powers that she would unlikely have had at that time.[26] Such misrepresentations of history do not help us grasp the nature of oppression or appreciate the varied means of resistance. The movie could have been inspired by John Dollard's images of interracial relationships in the 1930s, which also failed to consider the inequality of power between Black women and White men in the South.[27]

During most of the twentieth century, there were many myths about Black women as poor and immoral mothers, many of those images overlooking Black women's powerlessness and the way that they are involved in a web of constraints and obligations.[28] We need to know more about how Black women negotiated various settings without power. Fantasies that Black women had a range of choices that they did not really have do not help us appreciate their social location. Du Bois saw the suffering in the lives of women he knew personally and of those he knew about through the empirical work that he did. Their suffering was grounded in their lack of rights, the nature of market work, and the controlling images that permitted such exploitation, which together cast a shadow over Black women's relationships to family and community. What is the lens that currently denies Black women's suffering? If we consider the race, class, and gender hierarchies that shape Black women's lives, we can better see and address their suffering.

The second theme addresses Du Bois's observations about Black women's work. His observations illustrate how gender expectations are cultural constructions that reflect political and economic realities. Slavery marked Black women's lives, but their work experiences continued to differ from the expectations for White women who benefited from racial privilege and various degrees of class advantage. The economic realities in the early days of freedom meant that Black women could not be dependent upon men but must be economic actors in their own right. What was born of necessity, as the earnings and wages of black males were limited, emerged as an alternative path rather than a deviant lifestyle.[29] However, there were many tensions around work, because the lack of protection of private patriarchy meant that Black women and girls were vulnerable in labor markets stamped with hierarchies of race, gender, and social class. Du Bois's observations and interviews showed that he was keenly aware of the struggles of the Black family in the days after Reconstruction and in the early part of the twentieth century.

The American Negro Family documents that economic survival was possible only if all family members labored. Even then, survival was not ensured. If people owned the land they worked, it was still the labor of all family members that made it possible to move beyond poverty. In the country, fathers, mothers, and children worked; there might be age and gender divisions of labor, but at critical times everyone was in the fields. In 1908, there was market work for women in the city along with reproductive labor in the home. In fact, Atlanta families were similar to their rural counterparts, although the former lacked cotton and their children were more likely to go to school. In one Atlanta family, the mother sold "vegetables, chickens, and eggs, milk and butter to neighbors, wash[ed] and iron[ed] and sometimes cook[ed]" for others.[30] Data on the weekly earnings and expenditures of laborers showed women's contributions to their families' incomes. Although weekly earnings may have varied from forty cents to three dollars, income from women was essential in helping these laboring families survive.

Many of Du Bois's contemporaries thought that men should assume their rightful place and "protect" women. Du Bois acknowledged the oppression of women's work but also valued their economic contributions since their earnings brought goods into Black homes. Du Bois recognized that, rather than replicating or imitating the patterns of White families, Black women created an alternative family pattern. Writing in "The Damnation of Women," Du Bois considered Black women's employment to be an economic revolution. His reading of the 1910 census differed from the mainstream view that most often labeled the Negro pattern as deviant. "There was in 1910 two and a half million Negro homes in the United States. Out of these homes walked daily to work two million women and girls over ten years of age—over half of the colored female population as against one fifth in the case of white women. These, then, are a group of workers, fighting for their daily bread like men, independent and approaching economic freedom!"[31] Du Bois's observations meant that he approached the issue of employment for women from behind the veil, seeking to know what work meant in their community.

What kind of sociology can we do when we begin with the reality of people's lives? Rather than be guided by abstractions that do not address the structural foundation of expectations for women and men, scholars can focus on the realities of their situations. Obviously, during Du Bois's time, Black women needed wider educational and employment opportunities; they also needed the vote. In the era when Black women were devalued because they deviated from the roles of protected White women, Du Bois's view was different. He looked at the realities of oppression and how people struggled against various forms of injustice, observing how people shaped their lives with limited power and access.

Writing in 1920, when World War I had opened up new employment options for women, Du Bois attributed the increasing number of broken families not to new roles for women but to a new economic reality that required their contributions. He warned, "We cannot abolish the new economic freedom of women. We cannot imprison women again in a home or require them all on pain of death to be nurses and housekeepers."[32] By acknowledging not only women's contributions to their families but also the freedom that employment could give women from those families, Du Bois seemed to be aware of the complexities of women's ties to the institution of family.

The third theme is a complex one that examines Black women's roles in preserving family and community. Writing in 1920, Du Bois thought such efforts "laid the foundations of the great Negro church of today, with its five million members and ninety million dollars in property."[33] It was not just the Black woman's market labor that supported the family, community, and church, but her emotional energy, commitment, and direction. Deborah Gray White documents mutual aid and assistance among women during slavery.[34] In a later work, White examines how women continued in the face of twentieth-century oppression and struggled to work together for mutual aid, particularly in the church, and to do "good works and acts of benevolence."[35] Although these actions were good, we must look at the complex circumstances that Black women faced. Having emerged from slavery with what was considered by the dominant group a bad reputation, Black women had to take on many responsibilities, including achieving respectability. We cannot view their actions independent of the lens employed to view Black women. "As the linchpin of Negro pathology and cultural inferiority,"[36] Black women had to redeem themselves and the race. Such representations were a burden and placed Black women in a web of obligations and responsibilities.

During much of Du Bois's life, the politics of respectability were in vogue. He dressed impeccably, partly to challenge negative stereotypes. Black women had to face even more negative images. Writing about this phenomenon, Griffin sees the politics of respectability as "a sincere attempt to address the conditions of black people both internally and externally. It is marked by an attempt to instill dignity and self-respect while also challenging negative stereotypical images of African Americans."[37] This stance did not fully appreciate the power of racism, yet pushed individual conformity as a way to uplift the race. In the late nineteenth and early twentieth centuries, many women took on the task. During the era of Jim Crow, those who secured an education were explicitly socialized to uplift the race. Families who moved out of poverty as well as middle-class ones adopted strategies for Black women that "reflected concern for the equally important aspects of formal schooling, respectable behavior, self-assurance, self-discipline, and social responsibility"[38] that would lead to success in both the private and public spheres. Yet these collective and individual strategies did not consider the structural barriers women, even educated ones, faced as they worked for family and community. Actions that deviated from the appropriate roles of the time were understood in individualistic terms; that is, people used the language of choice rather than appreciating the limited range of options available to Black people.

It is often hard to appreciate the limitations of that range. Black families and communities have organized many of their activities to resist various forms of exploitation. These families have nurtured their children to grow up to work in various ways to shift the balance of power so that Black Americans will have access to work, rights, and a greater ability to shape their own representations of the community. Rather than automatically being sites for liberation, Black families and organizations can provide settings where Black women can face the complexities of both internal and external controlling images of themselves. Collins addresses this dilemma in noting that these settings can be "contradictory sites where Black women learn skills of independence and self-reliance that enable African American families, churches, and civic organizations to endure. But these same institutions may also be places where Black women learn to subordinate our interests as women to the allegedly greater good of the larger African American community."[39]

Politics and sentiments often dictate celebrating Black institutions, particularly the family, in light of negative stereotypes from the dominant group. However, we can be realistic in assessing how all settings are places to address both external and internalized oppression. What are the costs of preserving the family? What are the costs of neglecting the external factors that weigh on the lives of the family members? We can see Du Bois's insights into these questions in *The Souls of Black Folk* in chapter four, "Of the Meaning of Progress," where we follow Josie to understand the complexities of women's work for the family and community.

While a student at Fisk, Du Bois taught in a rural school in western Virginia for two summers. Fisk students were trained and then sent off to find a school where they would teach in the summer. It was Josie, who was eager for an education and who, upon hearing of Du Bois's quest for a place to teach, told him of the need for a teacher in her community. Josie "was a thin, homely girl of twenty, with a dark-brown face and thick, hard hair."[40] Du Bois spent the summers of 1886 and 1887 in her community with its young people and their families.

Du Bois observed the lives of rural families. He wrote: Josie "seems to be the centre of the family; always busy at service, or at home, or berry-picking; a little nervous and inclined to scold, like her mother, yet faithful, too, like her father. She had about her a certain fineness, the shadow of an unconsciousness and heroism that would willingly give all of life to make life broader, deeper, and fuller for her and hers."[41] Du Bois had great hope for his schoolchildren—students "such as Josie, Jim and Ben—to whom War, Hell and Slavery were but childhood tales, whose young appetites had been whetted to an edge by school and story and half-awakened thought."[42] Du Bois sees promise here, but also the obstacles. "And their weak wings beat against their barriers,—barriers of caste, of youth, of life, at last, in dangerous moments, against everything that opposed even a whim."[43]

This chapter in *The Souls of Black Folk* is a revision of an earlier essay written in 1899. The chapter includes his follow-up visit ten years after his summers in Virginia where we learn about the realities of adulthood for those promising young folks. Josie's gray-haired mother said simply, "We've had a heap of trouble since you've been away."[44] The family had endured crises and Josie was there to help them survive. Josie gave her brothers money perhaps to go to the North after one had been wrongly jailed. She helped the family sell the farm and move into town. She toiled a year in Nashville to furnish and make the new house a home. She worked as her sister brought a nameless child into the house. Josie's life was one of toil and sacrifice. She had given up the vision of school days and after one more disappointment, she died. Behind the veil, Du Bois saw the reality of Black women's work for the family and community. In other essays he celebrated their efforts, but there was a sober view here that acknowledged the web of obligation shaped by genuine commitment and love. At the end of the chapter, he wrote:

> My journey was done, and behind me lay hill and dale, and Life and Death. How shall man measure progress there where the dark faced Josie lies? How many heartfuls of sorrow shall balance a bushel of wheat? How hard a time is life to the lowly, and yet how human and real! And all this life and love and strife and failure,—is it the twilight of nightfall or the flush of some faint dawning day?[45]

Laboring for family was noble and, during much of Du Bois's era, this effort was critical for family and community survival. Yet we must acknowledge the complexities of the expectations of others and the concerns of individual women. In thinking about Josie, we can recognize Du Bois's appreciation of new work options for Black women during World War I. Prior to that time, Josie and other women in the South had few choices of jobs. Outside of farming, most women who lacked an education did domestic work. Josie did this work because she was expected to and because she wanted to care for her family. In the end, we have to recognize Josie's suffering and how it is related to her unique position in history. In the late nineteenth and much of the twentieth century, Black women worked and cared for families without legal rights and the franchise, particularly in the South. There were regional variations, but for many people educational opportunities were limited as segregation de jure or de facto made training for other work difficult. Segregation and job discrimination shaped where Black women could work. These forms of exploitation were accompanied by media representations that devalued Black women by communicating that they were satisfied with domestic work. A sociological perspective that recognized Black women's suffering, the role of the market work in their lives, and the complexities of their family and community ties would help us see and study them. We could see how their lives were constructed on a landscape of oppression based on race, gender, and social class. With this knowledge we would also be able to recognize the unique shape of their resistance, when they were successful and even when they failed.

If more sociologists had read Du Bois, even these early works, the study of Black women would have been more advanced in the field. In fact, my own travels in the field would have been different.

I want to conclude with a story that illustrates how those in the field of sociology had trouble "seeing" Black women. In the spring of 1974, I was a student in the first seminar in gender at Brandeis University. I was one of two students interested in researching women of color, a fact that our classmates found perplexing since they questioned what we could possibly learn from looking at devalued groups. After reading the little scholarship on Black college women on predominantly, or really overwhelmingly, White campuses, I interviewed Black women who were college seniors in 1974. I was struggling to develop a framework for my analysis.

Many of the raised working-class Black women had excellent high school records that earned them scholarships to prestigious institutions. They were pushed by families, who had high expectations of them, to take advantage of these wonderful educational opportunities at predominantly White colleges. Education was an investment in the future, not just an economic consideration, but these women would assume a role in aiding their families and communities.

However, life in these prestigious institutions in the 1970s was not easy. Many of the women found their surroundings unsupportive, and they had to prove themselves constantly because most students and faculty were either hostile or indifferent. These Black women carried the internal pressures of their token status; that is, they knew that they had to do well to keep the doors open for others. Yet their lives on campus were often lonely because they had little social life. An issue that I explored in the interviews was what these young college women did in the face of these challenges, tensions, and barriers. Many threw themselves into their work, postponing other issues until after college.

When I talked with my professor about these interviews to gain her help in framing an analysis, my professor said, "Oh, they act like men." To which I replied, "No, they just do not act like White women." Nor were they superwomen, which was a term used to describe educated Black women who tended to marry and raise families, a balancing act that was a new challenge for many White women in the 1970s. Black women should not be measured against White women, a stance that denies the reality of racism. They need to be appreciated within the context of their own social and historical experiences. Those seniors did not go away to college in the same way as middle-class White women of that era. They approached college knowing that they would be economically responsible for themselves and others and knowing that they would be tokens in many settings.[46]

Viewing Black women within the context of their own lives means acknowledging the suffering and sacrifices that Du Bois could see because their options, perceptions, and sense of responsibilities varied from those of their privileged White sisters. The field would have been deeply enriched if sociologists had paid attention to Du Bois's writing. Like others, I am pleased that many students and scholars are reading his words now and thinking about his contributions to framing an analysis of Black women's lives.

3

The Soul of The Philadelphia Negro *and* The Souls of Black Folk

Alford A. Young, Jr.

A remarkable quality of W. E. B. Du Bois's scholarship is that each of his works, especially those produced around the turn toward the twentieth century, are in direct and immediate conversation with the others. In fact, it might best be said that his body of work constitutes a series of interrelated conversations pivoting on a core problematic concerning race, the African American experience, and the prospects for black American social advancement. As historian Thomas Holt has argued, that problematic is framed by five central questions:

1. What (and how) does race mean?
2. How is it related to the larger history of humankind?
3. How does one study it?
4. How can one understand and overcome its pernicious effects on human life and aspirations?
5. How can race's pernicious effects on life experience and life aspirations be overcome?[1]

Thomas Holt provides one of many voices affirming that any attempt to make sense of Du Bois's overarching scholarly project must regard each of his works as standing in conversation with the others.[2] More specifically, Du Bois's writings reflect an intense commitment to revisit and sometimes revise his approach to ontological matters concerning race, the African American experience, and the experiences of other people who have been categorized as "black." Du Bois forwarded this agenda by applying and incorporating a wide-ranging set of methodological, epistemological, and empirical perspectives in his scholarship.[3] Hence, rather than viewing his work in terms of a pattern of linear development, it is more useful to think about his pursuits as constituting circular investigations of, and intersecting approaches to, the same concerns.[4]

This chapter embraces the idea that while each of Du Bois's scholarly products does stand alone as a critical piece of scholarship, there is significant merit in following Holt's and others' claims of assessing them as works in direct conversation with each other. Accordingly, the following pages pursue an ongoing discussion about the two most substantive and highly regarded of Du Bois's contributions during the turn toward the twentieth century, *The Philadelphia Negro* and *The Souls of Black Folk*. Each work represents a particular effort to document and interpret the quality of life for African Americans at the dawn of the twentieth century, and the particularities of each effort offer considerable space for comparative analysis.

The Philadelphia Negro (hereafter called *Negro*) was an effort to apply formal social scientific research techniques, especially ethnographic analysis, toward understanding the situation of African Americans. Du Bois launched the research endeavor underlying this project in the mid-1890s. He located it in Philadelphia's Seventh Ward, which was at that time the largest concentration of black Americans in an urban American community. This effort resulted in a vivid empirical description of the social dynamics relevant to the social condition of African Americans at that time. Alternatively, *The Souls of Black Folk* (hereafter called *Souls*) offered a more philosophical and exegetical commentary on the matter. Accordingly, this work offered more introspective accounts and analyses of that condition. Framing the relationship of these works in this way, however, only scratches the surface of how each complemented the other with respect to their mutual focus on the condition of African Americans at the dawn of the twentieth century.

Ultimately, *Souls* and *Negro* were products of the same enduring concern that Du Bois had about how black Americans are read and regarded as social beings in turn-toward-the-twentieth-century American society, both as a collective entity and as individuals. Although *Negro* was formally published four years prior to *Souls*, they essentially were contemplated, researched, and written in the same period of time.[5] Consequently, both works were products of a particular vision that Du Bois had of race, racism, and the condition of African Americans at the turn toward the twentieth century. That vision was rooted in Du Bois's quite personal and intense preoccupation with how he was situated as a black American, by both black and white Americans, given his unique childhood rearing in an overwhelmingly non–African American social milieu, his attendance at elite educational institutions, and his immersion into intellectual circles that were beyond the reach of all but a handful of African Americans during the late 1800s (and, in fact, for many decades thereafter). The conversation between *Negro* and *Souls,* then, is not figurative, but rather is one that literally began in Du Bois's head while he was doing this work. It was centered on his grappling with a threefold challenge of exploring the social and interactive dimensions of the African American condition in *Negro;* attempting to ascertain more fully the existential, emotional, and cognitive dimensions of that condition in *Souls;* and configuring more clearly his own relationship to other African Americans as well as the implications of his placement in the social category of black American.

Over the past century, the conversation between *Negro* and *Souls* moved from Du Bois's internal deliberations to debates occurring among scholars in academia. It would be both simplistic and incomplete to describe this later, considerably more public, conversation as constituted by the positioning of each work at opposing ends of scholarly inquiry into the African American condition (that is, as social scientific qua *Negro* and humanities qua *Souls*).[6] Rather, the conversation is of a more profound and complex nature. In part, this is because neither work was produced out of a codified paradigm for scholarly inquiry. Therefore, the prose contained in each work traverses freely across a range of intellectual and practical concerns. As *Souls* consisted of a collection of essays on various topics, this freedom is not at all startling and perhaps even expected. However, *Negro* was a product of a carefully crafted field study. Thus, the expansive commentary on the matters listed earlier position *Negro* as an especially intriguing text to consider alongside *Souls.*

The principal objective of *Negro,* as Du Bois posited in that book, was to illustrate the complexity and diversity of African American life to a public that regarded African Americans as a simple and unsophisticated mass of people that were ill-equipped to survive modernity (which was unfolding in the United States most explicitly in terms of a rapidly expanding industrial socioeconomic order). The most appropriate means for Du Bois to document such complexity was to concentrate on the social and interactive realms of life for black Americans. However, in both a political and intellectual sense, Du Bois's quest actually was even broader than this objective implies. That is, in addition to demonstrating the virtues of empirical research for framing and informing a logic for the social advancement of African Americans, Du Bois aspired to ascertain, as broadly and richly as possible, what constituted the existential dimension of the African American condition and how black Americans made sense of it while navigating their everyday lives. By "existential" I mean the deep, underlying convictions, attitudes, worldviews, and feelings that black Americans adopt or embrace as a result of their being socially classified in this racial category. It is in confronting this aim that *Negro* moves far beyond the expected tightly structured and focused empirical analysis.

Souls was a wholesale investment in exploring the existential dimension. As *Souls* was not bound to a formal empirical research design, Du Bois was much freer in this work to explore and elaborate upon his queries about the existential dimensions of the African American condition. Thus, *Souls* was a crucial tool for achieving the objective of asserting the humanity of black Americans. More importantly, this work provided him with the space to more fully uncover and explore that part of his project that was broached upon, but left quite unsettled in *Negro*.[7] Indeed, foremost among the myriad goals of *Souls* was the elucidation of the human capacities of black Americans as a complex group of thinking and feeling people. *Souls* achieved that end more directly by bringing together within a single volume the tools of literature, musicology, and social thought to make the case for the humanity of black Americans. In doing so, this work provided a heuristic for coming to terms with both the possibilities and limitations of *Negro* as a social scientific approach to understanding certain aspects of the social condition of African Americans.

In exploring the relationship of *Negro* and *Souls* around issues of the existential dimensions of the African American condition, this essay concentrates more directly on *Negro*. It especially considers what is revealed about Du Bois's use of ethnography as a tool to address, even if only preliminarily, the existential domain of the African American condition.

The motivation behind Du Bois's interest in discerning the existential dimensions of the African American condition, as well as the capacity for African Americans to reflect upon it, was twofold.

Politically and intellectually, he believed that doing this work would enhance the landscape for broad public comprehension, acceptance, and future scholarly exploration of the humanity of black Americans. His commitment to rescuing a notion of a complex black American self was a by-product of his studies with psychologist William James and others at Harvard University (where Du Bois completed his Ph D in 1895), who pushed forward the (at its time) radical idea that a complex sense of selfhood was a definitive property of each human being.

Du Bois was thoroughly committed to the notion that demonstrating that there was a domain of self-reflective consideration about the existential dimensions of African American life would provide evidence of the complexity of the humanity of African Americans. The second aspect of his interest was that Du Bois also was extremely preoccupied with understanding his own social location as an African American. While researching and writing *Negro* and *Souls,* Du Bois was very much in the midst of trying to make sense of not only what it means for black Americans to be socially categorized as such but also what it meant for him to be placed within this category. Hence, coming to terms with the existential dimensions of the African American condition was a step in Du Bois's personal (as opposed to intellectual) understanding of what it meant to be a black American.

This second aspect has a deep biographical foundation. Late in his life Du Bois wrote about his early childhood being a period of considerable intrigue over race. This was the case for him because he grew up as a lightly complected boy in a Massachusetts community that was home to very few African Americans in the mid-1880s.[8] This meant that race was an extremely subtle and mild property of his early life experiences. Having experienced a personal past absent of severe and consistent racial strife, Du Bois, and a number of his biographers as well, carefully chronicled what it meant for him to come into more complete recognition of the social pervasiveness and power of race as an adolescent and young adult. A major part of his doing so involved his struggle to make sense of what being classified as African American (or "Negro," as it was the term of his day) implied about him as a social being.[9] Hence, Du Bois was hungry to know, quite literally, what black Americans do, think, and feel because of, and in reaction to, their status in American society.

What they do comes through much more transparently in *Negro* as this work involved intimate and extensive ethnographic analysis.

How they think and feel, however, is a concern that is shared by *Negro* and *Souls.* Yet *Negro* demonstrates the limits of empirical investigation to deliver on the existential dimension, which consists of the deeper, most introspective aspects of such thought and feeling. *Souls,* in contrast, reached far beyond the boundaries circumscribing *Negro.* As the existential dimension of the condition of African Americans was at the forefront of *Souls,* many of its ideas and arguments do not simply encourage but demand a return to and rereading of *Negro* in order to advance an understanding of Du Bois's efforts as an empirical social scientist to approach the existential terrain.

By drawing upon some of the arguments and claims in *Souls,* then, this essay explores how *Negro* approaches, but cannot fully articulate, the existential dimensions of the African American social condition and the degree to which African Americans consider them. In doing so, this chapter elucidates how Du Bois's writing in *Negro* anticipates this shortcoming while illustrating how the empirical approach taken in that book essentially helped Du Bois to begin inquiring into a matter that he explored more fully in *Souls.* As will be argued in the following pages, he made considerable progress but, even after taking the argument in *Souls* into account, Du Bois did not come to closure on these questions.

Two Methodological Approaches to the Existential Dimensions of the African American Condition

Negro was Du Bois's most substantive effort to date to bring the tools of empirical social scientific investigation to bear on the social condition of African Americans at the turn toward the twentieth century. Accordingly, his investment in *Negro* was for the purpose of producing policy-oriented scholarship that would reveal the true condition of black Americans as well as chart a plan for their advancement in American society. A pioneering field study, *Negro* was Du Bois's effort to document the condition of African Americans in turn-toward-the-twentieth-century Philadelphia's Seventh Ward, then the largest African American residential community in the country (which housed more than 9,000 black Americans, or 20 percent of the African American population that was then residing in Philadelphia). *Negro* has become regarded as a classic text within scholarly communities dedicated to explorations of race theory and race relations. In part, *Negro* achieved that status because of the vast array of data

Du Bois garnered to investigate the life situations and prospects of black Americans in Philadelphia's Seventh Ward, including surveys, observations, and document analysis in the multimethod design that shaped this work. While the work defies description as the product of a single methodological approach, it is widely considered to be the first urban ethnography in American sociology.

Du Bois's exposure to empirical research emerged during his studies in Germany, where he was influenced by Gustav von Schmoller. In Germany he came to understand the analytical value of collecting data about individual social statuses and circumstances, aggregating it for the purpose of developing arguments about social groups and categories and providing an interpretive logic for it.[10] Consequently, in *Negro* Du Bois delivered a substantive analysis of African American life in that city, which, among other points of concern, shed light on the early phase of northern migration for black Americans, the social conditioning processes of urban life, the social institutions and lifestyles that were created there, and the enduring effects of slavery.

In delivering a comprehensive and penetrating assessment of Philadelphia's Seventh Ward, *Negro* introduced multimethod empirical research to the American intellectual landscape.[11] The research for *Negro* was conducted between August 1, 1896, and December 31, 1897. During that period of time, Du Bois carried out a house-to-house survey of 9,000 blacks living in the Seventh Ward. In order to conduct his research, Du Bois made use of six schedules for data collection. They included a family schedule (which documented the number of family members, sex, conjugal condition, and similar information), an individual schedule (which documented single-person data in the same manner as did the family schedule), a home schedule (which documented information about the number of rooms in each domicile, the amount of rent paid, the number of lodgers, and other related data), a street schedule (which documented information about each street and alley in the Seventh Ward), an institution schedule (which documented information about local organizations and institutions), and a house-servant schedule (which documented information about any house-servants living with their employers).

Du Bois also made use of data that he gathered about other city wards in order to document any striking demographic differences between these areas and the Seventh Ward. His ethnographical research involved door-to-door canvassing, public observations, minor studies conducted by the Abolition Society and Friends, the U.S.

Census Bureau, and reports published in local newspapers. He buttressed his analysis by incorporating into the material discussions of the history of African Americans in Philadelphia in order to flesh out more fully his assessments of their individual and social conditions and the physical and social environment of the Seventh Ward.[12]

In making his case in *Negro,* Du Bois presented an intricate, but also disturbing, weaving of class and racial effects in documenting the conditions of the Seventh Ward in Philadelphia.[13] In doing so, he argued that the urban slum was a symptom, and not a cause, of the economic, social, cultural, and political condition of African American urban life. He also argued that slavery, prejudice, and environmental factors were the principal causal factors affecting African American life in Philadelphia. This work resembles the kind of community-centered, fact-finding sociology that would appear on the American landscape in the following two decades (in large part because its proponent, and one of the early leaders of the University of Chicago school of sociology, Robert Ezra Park, also studied empiricism in Germany). However, aside from being the first of such studies to be produced in America, *Negro* remained a pathbreaking community study because it helped establish a vernacular for writing about the social conditions of black Americans, despite its moralistic claims and an elitist disposition taken toward lower-income black Americans.

As Du Bois's presence is vivid throughout the work, *Negro* continuously draws the reader toward intensive consideration of who the author is and what his intentions are for producing such a work. As he stated in the early pages of *Negro,* his aim for the study was to provide information that would guide the efforts to find solutions for the array of problems that African Americans confronted in the urban arena.[14] However, the work also makes clear that Du Bois determined that this study would also introduce and test the capacities of empiricism to uncover certain truths and postulates about black Americans, which would implicitly assist him along his own path of self-discovery about the social implications of being a black American. Hence, the pursuits in *Negro* were aimed at enriching not only white Americans' knowledge of black Americans but also Du Bois's own personal understandings about black Americans.

In comparison to *Negro, Souls* involved an altogether different approach to the situation of black Americans. However, the approach taken here did not largely concern itself with the visible dimension of African American life. Instead, *Souls* reached much more deeply into the existential domain. As the literary critic Shamoon Zamir argued, *Souls* is as much a journey into the unknown or half-known aspects of black life for Du Bois as it is for white Americans.[15] The journey taken in this work is broad and far-reaching given the range of topics and issues discussed in its pages.

In the book's fourteen chapters (and some minimal front and back matter), Du Bois employed literary techniques, sociopolitical commentary, and the presentation of lyrical verses and sheet notes to articulate a vision of African Americans as thinking and feeling people—that is, as human beings—who, by virtue of their social predicament as victims of America, demonstrate the failure of America to extend to them the post–Enlightenment era virtues of liberty, equality, and democracy. In the course of articulating this vision, *Souls* comments on a set of wide-ranging issues and concerns. One is the failing of sociologists (and, implicitly, empirically focused social scientists) to study African American life with sufficient integrity and depth. A second is the pitfalls and circumstances of post-Emancipation politics as they pertain to the mobility prospects of African Americans. A third is the crucial role of education in the process of racial uplift (which includes an explicit critique of Booker T. Washington's emphasis on manual training in lieu of higher learning). Fourth, he explores the political economy of the post-Emancipation South and its effect on African Americans.

More extraordinarily, though, in *Souls* Du Bois also aimed to reconstitute an understanding of the historical experiences of African Americans that does not simply attempt to place African American history in the public imagination, but more crucially and heroically strives to convey how consciousness is a product of historical forces and processes. As such, Du Bois ultimately argued in *Souls* that any effort to understand a group of people necessitates understanding how history has impinged upon and shaped their capacity to envision and express themselves, their social situation, and the ways in which people external to that group (in this case, obviously, white Americans) have affected these processes.

Souls is commonly regarded by scholars in race theory and African American intellectual history as something of an ur-text for investigating the social, intellectual, psychological, and political implications of race and the African American condition near the turn toward the twentieth century.[16] *Souls,* however, is much more than a seminal text in the history of African American letters. This work also informs analyses of present-day circumstances concerning race, racial dynamics, and the African American experience. After all, the problem of blackness—that is, the problems that both black Americans encounter in their efforts to become more fully included, accepted, and recognized as equal participants in American civic, political, and social life and that many white Americans have with coming to terms with the quests of black Americans to achieve these ends—remains an issue contemporarily as it did when *Souls* first appeared. This makes an effort to reconsider *Souls* more than just a project in intellectual history, but one relevant to the significant uncertainty and anxiety about the status of race, and the social condition of African Americans, in modern American life.

What Du Bois aspired to know about the reaction of black Americans to how white Americans situate and acknowledge them is a consistent point of concern in this work. Additionally, among its vast and complex objectives *Souls* provides an account of what Du Bois believed to be the limits for social scientific inquiry into the African American condition. In essence, *Souls* became the venue for dealing with those aspects of the African American social condition that the formal social science methods of observation and statistical accumulation (albeit crude as they were at the time of Du Bois's writing) could not unpack and explore. This work represents the counterapproach to the methodological orientation of *Negro*. Hence, the observational project in *Negro* gives way to the more abstract and contemplative consideration of the subjective dimensions of color prejudice that is delivered more fully in *Souls*.

The Beginning and Ends of the Empirical Research Methods for Grasping the Existential Domain

Negro was, quintessentially, a modernist scholarly project in that it aimed to involve the application of social scientific data to definitions and interpretations of social conditions and problems, and the means to solve them. However, Du Bois's efforts do not stop at a define-and-solve-the-problem orientation that would capture much of the mid-twentieth-century scholarly pursuits concerning race and African Americans. In addition to delivering a rich and provocative social scientific analysis of black Americans in this emergent metropolis, *Negro* broaches upon some theoretical and existential concerns about black Americans and the problematic of race in America that mere social scientific data collection and analysis do not allow him to fully illuminate and interrogate. Accordingly, this work aspired to move into deeper and richer discoveries of the social implications of race and the limits of social scientific inquiry for that objective, as much as it is about documenting problems and charting solutions for them.

As much as Du Bois aimed to advance an agenda for social research and policy concerning black Americans through his publication of *Negro,* he ultimately was limited by the epistemological boundaries of empiricism in social scientific inquiry. That epistemology did not allow him to effectively grapple with certain existential dimensions of blackness. Those dimensions concern the issue of what it feels like, at core emotional and cognitive levels, to be a black American. This concern was addressed in only preliminary fashion in *Negro,* and it was done so strictly in terms of Du Bois's giving his voice on the matter in an often self-questioning and always cautious style of writing. Accordingly, the very language that he employs in *Negro* reveals that he is unable to construct a satisfactory argument about what constitutes the inner feeling of being a black American. Hence, *Negro* reads as if, rather than closing in on an opinion about the matter, its author remained in the midst of discerning the range of effects and consequences of color prejudice on the lives of black Americans as an initial step toward posing a concluding opinion.

His own expressions of this hesitancy to draw firm conclusions on the matter appear throughout *Negro.* Indeed, they are implicated in his critical questioning of what can and cannot be conveyed through an empirical research initiative. For instance, in the third section of the book's first chapter, Du Bois explores issues concerning the credibility of the methods of data collection and analysis used to produce *Negro.* Here he points out that the best methods of sociological research are liable to inaccuracies such that findings must be presented with some measure of diffidence.[17] He goes on to argue further that the researcher "must ever tremble lest some personal bias, some moral conviction or some unconscious trend of thought due to previous training, has to a degree distorted the picture in his view."[18] In the portions of the project where observations of life in the Seventh Ward take center stage, Du Bois presents a cluster of problems concerning findings and analysis. He says in regard to this method that the sources of error occurring in the course of door-to-door investigations include misapprehension, vagueness, and forgetfulness on the part of the researcher in observing social life.[19] As for field interviews, Du Bois cautions that deception may be practiced by a respondent. The overall impact of these occurrences is that a researcher's conclusions become little more than inductions from "but a few of the multitudinous facts of social life, and these may easily fall short of being essential or typical."[20]

Contemporarily, these may appear to be rather common methodological points of concern for a researcher as he or she embarks upon a fieldwork project. However, for Du Bois the calling of attention to minimize the inclusion of personal biases and moral convictions in the course of analysis is done so graphically because Du Bois is mindful of and explicit about how much personal conviction drives his intentions for social research. He was highly conscious of his own racial position and classification as a "Negro" and the limits and misconceptions about him that came with it. He was intrigued by the power that racial ascription maintained in social life, especially because of the extreme stereotypes and misperceptions that were associated with the racial category of black American. Du Bois was equally conscious of his own intellectual agenda, which was to create ample space for the recognition of the humanity of African Americans and their capacity to contribute to societal advance in an emerging industrial arena. Hence, his statements do not simply convey his quest to be a responsible investigator of social life, but rather the foreground for what preoccupied his own thinking about how to properly situate himself and his intellectual and political interests in the study of race and the African American experience as he went about exploring the situation of African Americans in Philadelphia's Seventh Ward.

In making his case, Du Bois keenly illustrated his awareness that it is possible for him to "see" that which other observers may not in his study of his fellow African Americans. Of course, this is because what he saw was a product of his own existential orientation as a black American, which included not only his interest and objectives for studying black Americans but his rapidly evolving racial consciousness as he stove to come to terms with his social location as a black American. His racial consciousness was rooted in both his accepting that others in the social world would regard him as a black American and his own sense of self as being intellectually and culturally superior to most black Americans.[21] Accordingly, rather than simply stating that his vision of the social dynamics of the Seventh Ward was correct, in his assessment of method Du Bois posited that the possibility remained that there was no consistent "there" to be seen by all observers.[22] Instead, what is often seen is precisely that which the observer is looking for in the first place.

In Du Bois's case, he is clearly looking to forward an argument that cannot be reached solely by surmising from social science data. First, he wanted to frame a vivid account of the heterogeneity and richness of the African American community in the Seventh Ward as a means of affirming the humanity of its inhabitants (and, implicitly, black Americans more generally). Second, he wanted to peer into the hearts and minds of black Americans (beyond the degrees to which observational analysis and survey data would allow) to explore the deepest dimensions of their feelings about being black Americans. Some of what Du Bois aspired to see about black Americans, then, was well beyond the realm of the visible. Thus, he responsibly questioned that capacity of investigators to observe any aspect of reality from a neutral or pure position.

The emergent contradictions in *Negro,* therefore, appear by way of Du Bois's investment in intimate observation, or seeing people as they live their everyday lives, coupled with his awareness that this activity is inherently limiting in allowing for a more thorough envisioning of the very people being observed. That inability is, in part, due to the limited sight of the observer, which results from the observer's quest to remain sensitive to what he or she is looking for as opposed to what else may be there to be seen. It is also partly due to the inability of the observer to fully gauge all of what goes on in people's preparation to act in the social world. After all, much of that preparation is mental activity, which is always unavailable to literal observation with the naked eye. From the start, then, Du Bois wanted to make clear in *Negro* that both the observer and the act of observing are inherently riddled with impediments standing in the way of the quest to make sense of how people engage in everyday life. A not insignificant impediment has to do with what the observer may want to see (and possibly want to ignore, or not be sensitive enough to see), given what the researcher conceives as the political stakes and objectives involved in the research undertaking.

In taking all of this into account, it becomes clear that a number of issues were at hand for Du Bois in what may initially appear as simple and straightforward disclaimers about method. His most troubling concern was how the impediments and circumstances affecting research could prevent him from offering a robust and precise portrayal of the deeper sentiments held by African Americans about their lives, especially given that he was working to cripple the flawed portrayals of black Americans that were proliferating through American society. His writing in *Negro* reflects an investigator who eagerly wants to capture a sense of how black Americans get on with the project of living like everyday human beings despite the overt racist challenges to their status as functional people. More specifically, *Negro* is an attempt to confront the challenge of maintaining accuracy and precision in discussing "them" while understanding that such a project always involves some reflection about and discussion of "himself."

Du Bois's preoccupation with his own subjectivity most directly involved his effort to deal with the secondary agenda that he had in writing *Negro,* that concerning the existential domain. Although his discussion of method allowed him to raise some critical questions about the capacity to explore the existential dimensions of African American life, he nevertheless forged ahead with this objective in *Negro.* This effort appears quite vividly in the concluding section of one of his empirically rich chapters, chapter 14, entitled "Pauperism and Alcoholism," and then periodically throughout the next two chapters (chapter 15, "The Environment of the Negro," and chapter 16, "The Contact of the Races"), before being more fully explicated in the final chapter (chapter 18, "A Final Word").

A seemingly odd feature of the appearance of this kind of commentary in the conclusion to chapter 14, "Pauperism and Alcoholism," is that it comes at the expense of an explication of the data presented in the very body of that chapter.[23] This chapter begins with a presentation of a litany of tables and diagrams that indicate how many black Americans residing in the Seventh Ward were housed in jail, temporary residential shelters, or facilities for the mentally impaired. Du Bois then provides a list of reasons as to why a sector of the population in this ward was impoverished (creating categories such as "lack of work," "laziness and improvidence," "sickness, accident, and physical disability," and others to substantiate his argument) and a set of depictions of some of the social and economic circumstances encountered by lower-income families. The final portion of data introduced in the chapter consists of tallies of the number of visits made by Seventh Ward residents to various neighborhood saloons, and a series of estimates of how much money the residents spent in them. After presenting this material Du Bois goes on to argue that poverty in the Seventh Ward is a product of the particular history and condition of black Americans. He discusses how the legacies of slavery and emancipation were complex in that while some African

Americans benefited materially since that period, others succumbed to the intense pressures of trying to adapt to independent living in a competitive industrializing sphere. Finally, Du Bois also points to immigration as a source of increased competition for black Americans.

After such commentary, the chapter takes a sudden turn to a rather broad-based claim about the pernicious quality of the social environment circumscribing African American life. Here Du Bois emphasizes the significance of the end of slavery and emancipation as turbulent transformations of the pace and pattern of everyday living for many black Americans (even if these transformations appropriately were much desired) and of immigration as a causal factor for increased competition in the workplace. Du Bois then goes on to argue:

> To this must be added a third as great—possibly greater in influence than the other two, namely the environment in which a Negro finds himself—the world of custom and thought in which he must live and work, the physical surrounding of house and home and ward, the moral encouragements and discouragements which he encounters. We dimly seek to define this social environment partially when we talk of color prejudice—but this is but a vague characterization; what we want to study is not a vague thought or feeling but its concrete manifestations. We know pretty well what the surroundings are of a young white lad, or a foreign immigrant who comes to this great city to join in its organic life. We know what influences and limitations surround him, to what he may attain, what his companionships [*sic*] are, what his encouragements are, what his drawbacks are.[24]

He goes on to say:

> His strange social environment must have immense effect on his thought and life, his work and crime, his wealth and pauperism. That this environment differs and differs broadly from the environment of his fellows, we all know, but we do not know just how it differs. The real foundation of the difference is the wide-spread feeling all over the land, in Philadelphia as well as in Boston and New Orleans, that the Negro is something less than an American and ought not to be much more than what he is. Argue as we may for or against this idea, we must as students recognize its presence and its vast effects....[25]

Herein lies the emergence of Du Bois's turn toward explicit concern with the existential dimensions of the African American condition. His claim about the immense effect that the social environment must have on the thought and life of black Americans is the beginning of a repetitive—and, as we shall see, at points more substantive—engagement with black Americans' inner and deep feelings about what it meant to be a black American. As indicated in the previous quote, he first writes about such prejudice with a sense of cautious intrigue. Color prejudice is initially addressed as an odd and unwieldy artifact in American social life. In addition to referring to it as a vague characterization of the social environment within which black Americans function,[26] Du Bois states that it is an "indefinite" and "shadowy" phenomenon."[27]

Throughout the middle portion of *Negro,* extensive tables and graphs that portray the social demographic status of black Philadelphians in various occupational sectors and other social groupings are sandwiched within this form of commentary. Du Bois's interpretive remarks are rarely accompanied by extensive commentary from the residents of the Seventh Ward. Moreover, these interpretive remarks often run far ahead of, or away from, what is reflected by the data that were presented around these assertions. To be clear, this should not be taken to mean that Du Bois was wrong in his interpretation, nor that he always failed to provide interpretations that bore a direct relationship to his data. Instead, these seeming excursions about the troubled social condition of black Americans reflect Du Bois's passion and determination to explore their significance in a manner that his ethnography or survey data cannot fully sustain.

Du Bois argued that much of the meanings attributed to race, racism, and the behavioral responses of black Americans in light of this was a by-product of the recent transition of African Americans into the status of freed men and women in an urban sphere and the changing cultural, social, political, and economic circumstances concerning their arrival into such a status. However, rather than immersing the reader in a mass of extensive quotations from African American residents of the Seventh Ward, or richly detailed notes that describe the design and shape of public spaces, buildings, and structures, Du Bois consistently tells, in straightforward fashion, what matters to these people and why it does. Consequently, his interpretations, rather than his evidence, stand as *Negro*'s foremost statement about what race and racism mean in everyday life, and what is portrayed as racially inscribed behavior, for African Americans in turn-toward-the-twentieth-century Philadelphia.[28]

Much later in *Negro* he regards color prejudice as an indefinite term that comprises an element of everyday thought that black Americans are wholly preoccupied with while white Americans may give it less significant, if not fleeting, attention,[29] and ultimately, as a deeper and less easily described result of the attitude of the white population toward black Americans (which includes a "real or assumed aversion, a spirit of ridicule or patronage, a vindictive hatred in some, absolute indifference in others").[30]

Some of the most vivid accounts of how Du Bois struggled to make sense of how black Americans took stock of their condition appear in his continual revisitation of the topic of color prejudice. In doing so, Du Bois flirts with the concept of color prejudice in order to begin illuminating how African Americans make sense of their plight as subjugated people. In initially striving to keep focus on the larger social interactive emphasis of *Negro,* Du Bois presents his preoccupation with color prejudice by way of assessing how it became manifested in interracial interactions and social relations. Discussions of color prejudice allow Du Bois to push forward with his interest in determining the social consequences of the interface of black and white Americans at work, on the borders of residential communities, and in other social institutions.

Eventually, the matter is given direct attention in the first section of chapter 16, "The Contact of the Races."[31] Here Du Bois focuses most explicitly on color prejudice in the first section of this chapter, appropriately entitled "Color Prejudice." Here, in contrast to his earlier imprecision, he also provides a more tangible depiction of the phenomenon as he discusses the reactions that white Americans have to color prejudice as it affects black Americans:

> Negroes regard this prejudice as the chief cause of their present unfortunate condition. On the other hand most white people are quite unconscious of any such powerful and vindictive feeling; they regard color prejudice as the easily explicable feeling that intimate social intercourse with a lower race is not only undesirable but impracticable if our present standards of culture are to be maintained; and although they are aware that some people feel the aversion more intensely than others, they cannot see how such a feeling has much influence on the real situation or alters the social condition of the mass of Negroes.[32]

In summarizing what he learned and thought about the phenomenon of color prejudice through his analysis of the Seventh Ward, Du Bois says:

> Such is the tangible form of Negro prejudice in Philadelphia. Possibly some of the particulur [sic] cases cited can be proven to have had

extenuating circumstances unknown to the investigator; at the same time many not cited would be just as much in point. At any rate no one who has with any diligence studied the situation of the Negro in the city can long doubt but that his opportunities are limited and his ambition circumscribed about as has been shown. There are of course numerous exceptions, but the mass of the Negroes have been so often refused openings and discouraged in efforts to better their condition that many of them say, as one said, "I never apply—I know it is useless." Beside these tangible and measurable forms there are deeper and less easily described results of the attitude of the white population toward the Negroes: a certain manifestation of a real or assumed aversion, a spirit of ridicule or patronage, a vindictive hatred in some, absolute indifference in others; all this of course does not make much difference to the mass of the race, but it deeply wounds the better classes, the very classes who are attaining to that to which we wish the mass to attain. Notwithstanding all this, most Negroes would patiently await the effect of time and commonsense on such prejudice did it not to-day touch them in matters of life and death; threaten their homes, their food, their children, their hopes. And the result of this is bound to be increased crime, inefficiency and bitterness.[33]

Du Bois surmises that a core problem with color prejudice, then, is not merely that it exists but that many of those who proliferate it do not always admit to, or even recognize, its pervasiveness. This compounds the problem for black Americans in that a feature of their existential reality is that they face subjugation by others who are not always (and possibly never) aware that they are subjugating these people. Realizing and trying to make sense of this doubling of subjugation is a step further in the direction of both ascertaining the existential dimensions of the condition of black Americans and discerning what it is that black Americans actually have to consider when reflecting on those dimensions.

The accumulation of social statistics, which documented the standing of African Americans according to measures of employment, health, crime, and delinquency, and the chronicling of public behavior, which largely involved assessments of involvements in social activities, allowed Du Bois to formulate some understanding of the effects of color prejudice on African Americans' self-consciousness about their position in American society. However, these analytical approaches did not allow him to unravel and diagnose with full satisfaction how color prejudice affected the inner feelings of African Americans about being subordinated people. Essentially, in *Negro* Du Bois was unable to more fully discern certain subjective dimensions of color prejudice, especially those affecting African Americans' sense of self and social being. On these matters, then, *Negro* raised more questions than it could answer.

The need to more fully interrogate the far-reaching effects of color prejudice, meaning those that allude to the existential dimension of the African American condition, must be considered alongside Du Bois's interest in the social dynamics that enforce racial groupings and categorizations. After all, these forces also are products of color prejudice. Indeed, most of Du Bois's turn-toward-the-twentieth-century writings reflect intrigue with that which seemingly bounds African Americans into a definitive social category. More particularly, he aspired to determine the existential mechanisms that bound black Americans into a social group. The existence of color prejudice indicated that victimization was a part of the process, but it was the case that the reactions of black Americans to this victimization mattered as well. Both issues loomed on the horizon as Du Bois held fast to a desire to understand that which accurately defined the basis for African Americans' coherence into a social category. For Du Bois, the fact that all black Americans were victims of color prejudice, if nothing else, bound them into a social category. Also, the means by which they responded to it indicated for him some patterns of consistency and similarity. However, the field research in *Negro* does not provide the evidence in and of itself of what facilitates this condition or the responses to it. That is because the affective dimensions became manifest internally, in the thoughts of black Americans, and only secondarily in their behavior.

As *Negro* primarily was a statement about behavior, it could not do the work of addressing this affective dimension as fully as necessary. This did not prevent Du Bois from using *Negro* to make what became a partial case for explaining what the effects of color prejudice were and how they could be challenged. However, it is in *Souls* where these issues get more thorough attention.

Souls as a New Beginning for Grasping the Existential Domain

Souls comes into play in this matter because this work allowed Du Bois to occupy the position of a more unencumbered "seer" of the African American condition. In *Souls,* Du Bois was enabled to operate as a seer who was not bound by the emerging formalities of social scientific inquiry. Du Bois positioned *Souls* as the space in which to extrapolate upon his criticism of what the social science observer claims to see that others may not. This work situated him as a mediator between the seen and unseen of African American communities because, unlike with *Negro,* Du Bois was fully able to break from the constraints of ethnographic inquiry, which is often predicated on an "invisible" seer who does not intrude with interpretations or analysis that cannot be directly grounded in the social dynamics of field settings.[34]

In *Souls* Du Bois was able to avoid questioning whether he could be true to his observations and documentations because this work involved an inward focus where he could more assertively posit himself and his personal queries as the basis for making claims about African Americans. Of course, as will be explained, Du Bois engaged new and different problems in *Souls* precisely because of the limits of positing himself as the exemplar of the situation of African Americans as a collective entity. Moreover, whereas Du Bois was cautious in *Negro* about where he stood relative to the so-called data, the writing in *Souls* reflects much less doubt and hesitancy.

In his assessment of *Negro,* literary critic Shamoon Zamir notes that because Du Bois is concerned with the fact that the so-called scientific authority of the researcher is invariably challenged by subjective orientation and introspection, he aspired to give ample time to introspective analyses of the African American condition.[35] *Souls* represents that effort. It is there that Du Bois can explore with intensity and depth, as philosopher Tommy Lott explained, "the operation of will in human action."[36] This is so because Du Bois realized that the bases for action, or agency, cannot be fully realized through formal social science investigation. Instead, one must come to terms with what Zamir labeled as the "deep structures of meaning" that are reified by reflective consciousness.[37] No means of observation or accumulation of statistics can carve out a space to wrestle with reflective consciousness because the latter is not visibly accessible. It cannot be captured by such research approaches, which depend on visible social activity and simplified reportage on it via survey instruments. Rather than applying such modes of analysis, psychological interrogation is the more appropriate tool for this kind of inquiry.[38] Accordingly, in the first chapter of *Souls,* entitled "Of Our Spiritual Strivings," Du Bois introduced this mode of investigation.

As this chapter of *Souls* was a revision of a piece previously published, it is clear that Du Bois was wrestling with some of the shortcomings and inadequacies of formal social science research methods for peering into the deepest sentiments of African Americans prior to publishing *Negro*. The shortcomings largely remain in the limitations of observational analysis. In *Negro*, Du Bois repeatedly pointed out how black Americans were affected by color prejudice at work and in regard to matters concerning public interaction. Yet, lurking behind all of these references was an intrigue about and questioning of what may be going on in the minds and hearts of black Americans given their victimization through pervasive color prejudice. In these moments Du Bois struggles to state and elaborate upon that which he observes—the despair, frustration, and anxiety resulting from racism. Yet, as all of these reactions are products of deeper feelings and impulses, Du Bois is also quite conscious of the fact that while explaining the behavioral reactions of black Americans, he could not convey all that results from the social condition of being discriminated against. Much of this is internal and, thus, unseen. As such, it falls beyond the purview of ethnography as Du Bois has employed it. A lingering concern for him, then, is how to tell a tale about that which was not literally seen but relates wholeheartedly and entirely to that which is visible.

The commentary in the first chapter of *Souls*, which was, in effect, a different kind of commentary about the effects of color prejudice than that found in *Negro*, is centered in both Du Bois's discussion of what it means for black Americans to account for their social existence by virtue of their being regarded as a social problem and by his introduction of the notion of a double consciousness. That latter concept defines for Du Bois the lens that African Americans adopt on the very social world within which they are regarded as a problem.[39] In *Souls*, Du Bois argues that the social world allows African Americans "no true self-consciousness, but only lets him see himself through the revelation of the other world."[40] He goes on to say that this sense of double consciousness "is a peculiar sensation ... this sense of always looking at one's self through the eyes of others.... One ever feels his two-ness—an American, a Negro; two souls, two thoughts, two unreconciled strivings; two warring ideals in one dark body, whose dogged strength alone keeps it from being torn asunder."[41]

As many have commented, the term *double consciousness*, especially as Du Bois conceived of and applied it, is riddled with problems. It was applied to many wide-ranging and diverse aspects of African Americans' inner thinking about themselves and American society. In an insightful essay, Dickson D. Bruce Jr. argues that the idea of a double consciousness served three purposes simultaneously for Du Bois. First, it referred to the power of white stereotypes in African American life, meaning that black Americans were positioned to be aware of what white Americans thought of them and aware that their self-thought could radically differ from it.[42] Second, double consciousness was a reference to being excluded from American society while still holding, however tenuous, the status of being an American.[43] This spurred in African Americans a conflicting internal drive to reconcile what being "African" was from being "American." Third, and most politically relevant, was the reference to a distinctive African consciousness that consisted of spirituality, exemplified by faith and suffering, and that was defined as culturally African in origin, in comparison with an American consciousness of materialism and increasing commercialism that was the emerging bedrock of American industrial-order culture.[44] The double consciousness of the African American was exemplified here by his or her standing in the midst of, and thereby embracing, both cultural patterns.

Furthermore, in another critical assessment of the term, Ernest Allen Jr. went further by stating that double consciousness was a simultaneous reference to the thoughts, strivings, aims, and ideals of African Americans. In reference to "Of Our Spiritual Strivings," he posed the question of whether the term was invoked to allow Du Bois to speak to the possible internal conflict that black Americans experienced over the internalization of contemptuous ideas that others in American society had of the African American presence, or whether it pertained to the conflicting thoughts, strivings, and ideals that black Americans held concerning the most appropriate means and mechanisms of social advancement in American life.[45] Allen argued, and I concur, that Du Bois does not settle on this matter. Allen eventually concludes that the concept of double consciousness was a flawed and imprecise means of encapsulating the tensions experienced by elite African Americans, the only segment of the African American populace that had both the capacity and desire to think about (and, consequently, was frustrated by the inability to achieve) social acceptance by white Americans.[46]

For Allen, it was this sector of the African American community that faced most directly the challenge of the direct and consistent refusal of white Americans to acknowledge African Americans' full rights as American citizens, while also demanding that they uphold the responsibilities of citizenship.[47] Black Americans whose labor prospects were restricted to sharecropping, laboring, household servitude, and other lower-tier work had no sustained interaction with white Americans that would result in intensive preoccupation with either a white American consciousness or an African-centered consciousness of any sort. Rather than experiencing any internal conflict about one's relationship to Africa, black Americans at the lower tiers of the American socioeconomic hierarchy remain preoccupied solely with attaining the means for economic survival, and for achieving some measure of material equality now that slavery had concluded (although the rise of legally sanctioned segregation in the Jim Crow South certainly posed further problems for achieving the latter objective).

The sociopolitical implications of double consciousness are that it refers to both alienation and the capacity for human action (even if action in this case is taken to mean the capacity of black Americans to see themselves in ways that white Americans are unable to). For Du Bois, the capacity to envision oneself and one's group standing is an indication of one's valid claims to membership in the human race. Hence, Du Bois's presentation of this effort to envision is an attempt to garner white American recognition of the humanity of black Americans.[48] However, a crucial problem remains in how Du Bois carried out this presentation. The problem remains in that only African Americans who share his privileged status are positioned to entertain esoteric thoughts about whatever may be some essence or foundation of blackness, and it is the entertaining of such thoughts that is a precursor to the emergence of a double consciousness. Thus, Du Bois's effort to ground the existential dimension of the black American condition collapses into a self-referential commentary on the matter. In other words, Du Bois answers the question of what the inner feelings must be of being a black American by asserting only what his inner feelings happen to be. *Souls* is a failure in the effort to derive any sense of a homogenous inner feeling.

Du Bois remains on much safer ground by approaching homogeneity in terms of the social problem resulting from, and constituted by, the African American presence in American society (which actually is quite well framed by the data presented in *Negro*). However, even that problem becomes manifest in the minds of African Americans in highly class-specific ways (such that the African American business owner realizes the problem in much different ways than does the African American sharecropper).

Du Bois's writing about both black Americans' feelings of their being a problem and their possession of a double consciousness was a bold attempt to define the contours of being an African American.[49] The existence of a double consciousness was an indication of the complex cognitive capacities of black Americans. The recognition of this complexity, by both black and white Americans, placed black Americans on equal footing with white Americans and, thus, legitimated their humanity. Thus, the term highlighted a problem that black Americans faced in American society while also affirming their legitimacy as full and equal members of that society. However, the fact that Du Bois applied this concept to these three very different and distinct social phenomena in the course of a single publication highlights his own incomplete effort to define with precision exactly what existential commonalities there were for black Americans. Yet doing so provides some depth of understanding behind Du Bois's claim that underlying blackness is a degree of yearning that serves as one of its common features.

The effort in *Souls* is largely one of emphasizing some presumably common existential features of blackness in the Western world. This is evident upon encountering the very first paragraph of the first essay, entitled "Of Our Spiritual Strivings," where Du Bois poses the following question: "how does it feel to be a problem?"[50] This ontological grounding of blackness as, quite literally, a problem is an effort in *Souls* to document that which affects all African Americans by virtue of their being located in the very social category of black American. The problem, as he defined it, is one of how difference becomes a property of social life and, ultimately, a source of social disdain. All black Americans are regarded as different, and, consequently, less worthy of assuming the category of human being as a result of being so regarded. Precisely because they are regarded as such, they must live a social existence as being, first and foremost, a problem.

One way in which Du Bois tries to flesh out the existential side of living as a problem is his writing in *Souls* about African American life as encapsulated within a veil. The notion of the veil appears almost immediately at the beginning of the book, in the fourth paragraph of the first chapter, where he spoke of the Negro as "a sort of seventh son, born with a veil, and gifted with second sight in this American world...."[51] This veil, which is referred to no fewer than twenty times throughout the book, is not simply an indicator of an explicit racial divide in American society, but rather of a divide that allows those outside the veil—white Americans—to look at those within it in ways that obscure more accurate, precise, or complex readings of such people. Those within the veil—black Americans—have no clouded vision of the social world, in particular, of how they are being read by those beyond the veil. The powerful existential significance of this is that a depiction of black Americans as a constituency encapsulated by a veil gives a precise and durable meaning, without falling back upon a biologically essentialist argument, about African Americans as to who this group of people happens to be and why they can be identified as a collective entity.[52]

As Kirt H. Wilson explained, the veil gives rise to a form of knowledge about one's social location in the eyes of others.[53] Hence, the pervasiveness of color prejudice results in a form of awareness and, potentially, agency for black Americans that is not readily apparent in public behavior (and this is beyond the purview of the ethnographic analysis in *Negro*). However, it becomes manifest through black Americans' understanding that, because of their subjugation, they are capable of seeing the world differently from white Americans, and white Americans lack the immediate understanding that black Americans may possess such a different vantage point on that world. That capacity for viewing the world differently, which for Du Bois is an existential quality, is also an affirmation of a particular selfhood that black Americans possess that helps position them as legitimate members of humanity.

Of course, one can raise a series of critical questions about the extent to which all African Americans stand behind a veil or, if so, whether they stand in the same place behind it. As with other matters, *Souls* does not provide the means for answering this question. What it does do, however, is introduce a vocabulary about the existential dimension of the African American condition and an argument about some of the circumstances and issues that surfaced in *Negro* but that could not be explored as fully in a formal social scientific study.

To do full justice to the various ways by which *Souls* elaborates upon or modifies the claims made in *Negro* would necessitate another essay. Accordingly, this essay only addresses some of the most vivid moments where *Souls* serves to unpack some of the unresolved tensions and queries appearing in *Negro*. Rather than fully explore the theoretical and epistemological foundations of *Souls* (which is the objective of many of the scholars discussed in this chapter's second endnote), portions of that book were referred to in this essay solely for the purpose of encouraging renewed thinking about Du Bois's effort in *Negro*. Hence, as stated earlier in this chapter, the objective of this contribution on the conversation between *Souls* and *Negro* centers on the soul of Du Bois as the author of *Negro* and, simultaneously, as a critical thinker about the possibilities and limits of social scientific inquiry. The works previously cited, as well as the additional chapters in this volume, more fully explore the intellectual and political project of *Souls*.

Conclusion

As an ethnographic study informed by a range of statistical data and historical information, *Negro* leaves little space to explore the psychological and philosophical terrain that pertains to these existential dimensions more fully elucidated in *Souls*. Yet, as the pages of *Negro* reveal, Du Bois's pursuit of an intimate, ethnographically informed study motivate him to delve into issues and concerns associated with such existential dimensions. However, the very research design of *Negro* did not allow him to complete this part of his agenda. In *Negro,* Du Bois quite conscientiously acknowledged how the empirical research tools that he employed allowed him to begin raising, but not fully answer, the question of what constitutes the existential dimensions of the African American condition near the turn toward the twentieth century.

Indeed, some measure of this resulting effect was due to the fact that when writing *Negro,* Du Bois was operating years ahead of a crystallized tradition of urban ethnography. Essentially, there were no rules about how to analyze and interpret fieldwork data or how to apply statistical evidence and measures to observational findings. Hence, rather than applying a codified set of rules and procedures for empirical research, Du Bois had to create his own template. Given Du Bois's strong interest in foregrounding the inner feelings of black Americans on race, racism, and racial interaction—all done in the effort to document their existential condition—he let his interests and curiosities direct his writing such that it provided an interpretive logic that, at many points, stood apart from his data, which were largely descriptive of the class standings, social activities, and interests of black Americans in Philadelphia's Seventh Ward.

Negro reveals the tensions resulting from Du Bois's effort to describe and interpret various dimensions of African American social life, review the effects of history on it, imagine a better future for these people, and envision his role and position as an African American communicator—attempting all of this for the readers of his work while also trying to unpack some notions of the existential dimensions of the African American condition. In pursuing each of these ends, *Negro* embraced a wide range of analytical projects beyond the mere focus on social life in a field site. Incorporating such breadth and depth mandated that the effort to construct a balanced and thorough argument on all of the stated grounds would be challenging. Achieving that end is made all the more complex by Du Bois's consistent intervention into this work by way of his moving far from the data in order to articulate some claim or commentary. In this way, he becomes a central point of focus in this work as much as does the research agenda. Du Bois's presence in *Negro* looms large because he assertively writes himself into the work by offering a strong interpretive voice for what African Americans think and do in their everyday lives.

Again, this should not necessarily be taken to mean that his data contradicted his interpretations. Instead, Du Bois often presented claims and arguments in *Negro* about the social condition of black Americans that maintained a distant relationship to much of the actual evidence that he accumulated during his fieldwork. However, his fieldwork in the Seventh Ward of Philadelphia provided him with the means to sharpen his points of focus concerning those dimensions. Ultimately, *Negro* did not settle exclusively on the analysis of the social and interactive dimensions of the African American condition. In fact, Du Bois's desire to explore this issue in *Negro* often led him to abandon strict emphases on his fieldwork findings and the information provided by his tables, graphs, and other data. Instead, in this work he repeatedly diverged into extensive commentary about what it feels like to live as a black American. This commentary was partly polemical (in order for Du Bois to best forward his explicitly political objectives) and partly the result of Du Bois's inventory of his own sensibilities and convictions about being a black American. Thus, a great deal of the interpretive content of *Negro* is not about the data themselves but is centered on exploring a question to which his data are only loosely connected and, hence, are not fully suited to help him answer.

Clearly, *Negro* provides the most robust attempt at that stage of Du Bois's career to compose a study reflecting the virtues of a social scientific inquiry. However, *Souls* allowed Du Bois to investigate the social effects of color prejudice in different, albeit related, dimensions altogether. *Negro* certainly provided Du Bois with the means to define, measure, and document various aspects of the social condition of African Americans. *Negro* also enabled him to discuss how various aspects generated, or at least affected, the emergence of others. What *Negro* could not do, however, was allow Du Bois to capture the feeling of being a black American, as statistical measures and responses to formal interview questions did not bring him very far into that kind of discovery. It simply was not enough to document that African Americans lived in the same geographic terrain (Philadelphia's Seventh Ward) or that, by virtue of such a residential arrangement, they must consistently interact with each other in public as well as private settings. What made the case for Du Bois about homogeneity for black Americans could not be found in the study of their patterns of social interaction but in the inner convictions maintained by them as a result of the sensibilities that white Americans had about them. Hence, *Negro* remains an exposé on African American life in terms of the social organization, patterns, and public behaviors of African Americans. There he introduces color prejudice as a major point of concern, and he begins to address, ever so tentatively, its effects on the psyche and behavioral pursuits of black Americans. However, one must turn to *Souls* to find the fruits of Du Bois's efforts along those lines.

Du Bois's ultimate inability to allow the data to tell certain aspects of the kind of story that he wants to in *Negro* gives way to his explicit effort to present *his* interpretation in *Souls*. This interpretation is one centered on the innermost feelings about being a black American. However, that work was, in fact, largely a statement about what Du Bois feels like as a black American because, as a work that is not empirical in the way that *Negro* is (that is, it does not draw upon collected accounts or testimonies of others), he is not positioned to tell any other story in its pages. Hence, he can deliver an argument only about the subjective dimensions of the African American condition that largely fall back upon his own particular experience of that condition, which is uniquely marked by his being a highly educated and privileged member of that social group.

Taken together, then, *Negro* and *Souls* represented Du Bois's most thorough application of analytical methods to date to document and investigate the social implications of racism for black Americans (most often defined in *Negro* as "color prejudice").

Consequently, in examining how these two works converse with each other, it becomes possible—indeed critical—to advance an argument about the limits of field research for understanding the full range of effects of racism on black Americans. Doing so has demonstrated how Du Bois grappled with both the possibilities and inadequacies of empirical social science for unearthing certain subjectivist dimensions of that phenomenon.

4

Cultural Politics in the Negro Soul

Charles Lemert

In the century since *The Souls of Black Folk* first appeared, much has changed. But not much has changed more than culture—its nature, its media of deployment, its role in the scheme of material and political things, its status as subject of interest and controversy in the academy. Yet, along the course of the change, it is seldom noted that W. E. B. Du Bois could well be considered a founder of culture studies—a right due him for one reason above others.

More than any before him, more even than many who would follow his lead, Du Bois understood that, in actual social history, there was no such thing as *culture* as such. Culture is always necessarily *cultures,* an unsettled plurality. *The Souls of Black Folk* in 1903 is, thus, a kind of manifesto before the fact of a general theory of culture as cultures, the effect of which would not come fully to light until the years following Du Bois's death in 1963 when the gathering force of the colonized world's resistance would sweep into the cultural centers of the European hegemony. It was then, in the middle years of the 1960s, after Du Bois's final affirmation of black nationalism in the move to Ghana, after the ironic implosion of the integrationist civil rights movement in the land he quit, that political and cultural conflict would begin to dismantle the civilization ideal of the European Diaspora.

The very idea that culture could be both singular and universal was foundational to the aspirations of the European Diaspora to be the fulfillment, if not quite the end, of human history. The ideal of continuous progress toward the Good Society required, of course, a convincing claim that, at the least, the modern world was different from all others before it. In political terms, the claim demanded a reason to trust that, when social evil occurred, it occurred as a sad but necessary entailment of progress toward the Good. Hence the prominence, if not quite triumph, of the utilitarian ethic, of assimilationist social policies, of the liberal project, of history as the history of the human, of humanism as a cultural style, of consumption as a sign of personal worth, among other well-known features of modernity's cultural apparatus. Or, to put it harshly, in order for the European Diaspora to sustain its sense of civilizational superiority, it had no choice but to exaggerate the singular universality of its values in order to draw attention away from the brutality of its colonizing methods. To this end, culture could not but be a principal topic and resource of true modernity.

Du Bois was on to the game, which he learned to play at Harvard and Berlin and enjoyed the rest of his life. Still, though he was famously devoted to European culture, Du Bois just as famously refused to obey the rules by which it was played on the manicured fields of its privileged schools. Before Harvard and Berlin, he passed the formative years of his late adolescence in the American South at Fisk from 1885 to 1887. There he lived for the first time on the black side of the veil and nowhere more so than in the summers among the isolated poor in the mountains of rural Tennessee. There he taught the poorest of the poor. The experience gave Du Bois the gift of second sight by which he saw the duplicitous truth of European civilization—its insistence on perfect adherence to its cultural program as the price for admission to its segregated peanut galleries. This is the modern colonizer's method—overwhelm the locally deviant cultures with the trinkets of civilizational benefit; offer the promise of cultural Progress as balm for the pain of its denial. "How shall man measure Progress there where the dark-faced Josie lies?" These words from "On the Meaning of Progress," the fourth essay in *Souls,* were the benediction pronounced on Josie, the most memorable of his summer-time pupils from the mountain village, who died before achieving the promises of adult life. Very real in the experience of his youth, Josie also stood for the rural poor in the mountains of eastern Tennessee—for, that is, those who taught him the true meaning of the Black soul of the American Negro.

Du Bois always measured the worth of Europe's singular culture against the suffering of those whose pain was covered by its pieties. He was never a romantic, ever a political realist. The genius of his cultural politics lay in the ability to enjoy the game of Europe's cultural arrogance, without underestimating the evil it inflicted. He was *in,* but not *of.* By planting Europe's cultural ideals into the dark soil of American Negro culture, Du Bois allowed for what, in later years, others would insist on—that cultures are always local, hence necessarily different, hence always political. When cultures come into contact with each other on the borders and battle lines of social differences, they always rub each other the wrong way. In the friction, the surface enamel erodes, the unruly irrupts. Against the rough edges, the cultures grind away, each and every one seeking its advantage, which is the very purpose and nature of politics.

There are two mistakes commonly made by those who read *The Souls of Black Folk* too quickly, with too much attention on the famous first essay, too little on the rest. One mistake is to take the double-consciousness idea as a psychology. The other is to take the talented tenth strategy as an elitist philosophy. In fact, double consciousness is a psychology only by way of being first a theory of cultures; the talented tenth is a philosophy only by way of being a cultural politics necessary for a time when the several millions freed in principle in 1863 were, by 1903, only marginally better equipped for the industrial age.

Du Bois's notoriously elitist personal style encourages the mistakes. He meant, to be sure, to put himself—both the individual and the icon he intended to be—at the junction of the theory of culture and the politics of cultural training. Anyone who feels himself called to be the moral representative of a people must be touched with a degree of self-importance. Still, it is a fact that Du Bois was the first modern Negro intellectual in America in that he, more than anyone before, and few since, was certifiably talented and well enough certified to stand at the border of the two cultures. "It is a peculiar sensation, this double-consciousness, this sense of always looking at one's self through the eyes of others, of measuring one's soul by the tape of a world that looks on in amused contempt and pity"—not a psychology, but a consciousness of the cultures in conflict. Du Bois's Negro was never of one mind; nor was he reducible to consciousness in the psychologizing sense of the word.

Du Bois's two souls are far more than the articulating elements interior to the "unreconciled strivings" of the Negro psyche. Though the double-consciousness theme may well have been borrowed by extension from his friend and teacher William James, mixed, no doubt, with the German idealism he learned in Europe, the theme is better understood by reference to the figurative measure by which Du Bois imposed order on a collection of essays. Du Bois was never a psychologist or a particularly devoted idealist in the philosophical sense. He was, however, nothing if not a race-man for whom, in Cornel West's phrase, the cultural politics of differences were first and foremost. From the early writings of which *Souls* was the high point, through the early work in the NAACP, to the Harlem Renaissance, including his editorship of *Crisis* magazine from 1910 to 1935, his politics were cultural politics. If with *Black Reconstruction* in 1935 he became, in Manning Marable's phrase, more the radical democrat and socialist, his politics remained to the very end those of a man of black culture. *Dusk of Dawn,* in 1940, may not have been quite so eloquent as *Souls,* but what it lacked in Victorian lilt it gained in a more parsimoniously tough poetic style—of which the finest expression is the dusk-of-dawn figure in the book's fifth essay where he turns his own first coming to the dark continent to the dawning light.

As is fitting for a self-made icon of the new Negro intellectual, Du Bois's life's work is best understood less as an early culturalist attitude that turned materialist in later years than as a continuous effort both to rein in and to give the lead to the powerful tensions he wrote of in *Souls.* From the first, the necessary cultural tension of the consciousness of the American Negro inescapably became a politics of "the warring ideals in one dark body, whose dogged-strength alone keeps it from being torn asunder." Hence, the man's dogged strength in the wars with the Tuskegee Machine, with the elitist elements in the NAACP, with the American government's war policies, with the anticommunist inspectors. His strength lay in the ability to change with the times while, again, keeping Josie as the fixed star of Negro purpose. The dogged strength lay in the gift of second sight he symbolized in the coupled epigrams that provide the integrating theme to *Souls*—lines of poetry from European culture; unmarked lines of musical notation from American Negro culture.

For Du Bois there was no such thing as culture—singular, exhaustive, and all-encompassing. All cultures are real, local, hence plural. That there could be such a thing as cultures—different, divided, and warring—could have occurred only to one in his position and only to such a one with the intellectual force both to see and to seize the tensions. Against the essentializing values of modern culture, Du Bois set the specific politics that arise in the differences. Negro consciousness for Du Bois was the consciousness of a global figure—"a sort of seventh son, born with a veil, and gifted with second sight in this American world." The warrant for thinking of Du Bois himself as elitist was the arrogant manner with which he played out the game as the Negro intellectual—a cultural presentation both demanded by his dealings with white culture and put on by the effects of those dealings on his intellectual and cultural work. As for the work itself, it was always cultural work done with Josie in the mind's eye. No fair reading of a book like *Souls* can lead to any other conclusion. But, then, no one said the world is fair, least of all along the color line where Du Bois positioned himself as *the* Negro intellectual—an unthinkable figure on both sides of the veil. American Negroes had, in 1903, seen too few; all but a few American whites could see any at all.

The very idea of the Negro intellectual is a disturbance on the tranquil scene of Western culture where culture, in all its several expressions, is normally thought to be an achievement of the unqualified human spirit or, among the analytically minded, at least a high-order governor that manages social disorder. None put the attitude better than Matthew Arnold in 1869 in *Culture and Anarchy*—an essay written because Arnold felt that culture had to be put right just when the modernizing world of industry, class conflict, and discord was putting culture, as he and his kind understood it, in serious doubt:

> Culture looks beyond machinery, culture hates hatred; culture has one great passion, the passion for sweetness and light. It has one even yet greater!—the passion for making them *prevail*. It is not satisfied till we *all* come to a perfect man; it knows that the sweetness and light of the few must be imperfect until the raw and unkindled mass of humanity are touched with sweetness and light.[1]

Arnold's emphasis on *all* is one of the signs of the extent to which he meant to purify culture against the corruptions of the cultures of the "raw and unkindled mass." Only culture as such, perfectly sweet and unglossed by the filth of human differences, could protect the West from anarchy.

In 1868, the year before Arnold's *Culture and Anarchy*, W. E. B. Du Bois was born in Great Barrington, Massachusetts. There he grew up in the white world's cultural ideal of universal perfection. There he learned to desire Harvard and Europe. There, too, he encountered the confusing sting of white exclusion, the full moral meaning of which he took from the lessons of Negro culture that he learned at Fisk and in Josie's Tennessee hills. Had he not spent those early years in the American South before the sojourns at Harvard and Berlin, he almost certainly would not have fashioned the theory of culture that ties together the several subjects and essays in *The Souls of Black Folk*, to say nothing of the ever more various and stunning works that would follow. In effect, *Souls* was the prolegomenon to a manifesto for Negro culture as the counter-soul of the true culture Arnold thought was one and indivisible.

But what are culture studies? How are they distinguished from the social study of other social things? Why are they not the same as literary theory or the sociology of culture? Why are such recent innovations as cultural sociology a pathetic substitute for the admittedly silly sociologies of culture? Culture studies are the study of cultures, plural. They are themselves various and multiple. If they have a precursor, it is cultural anthropology wherein differences are at the methodological heart of social things. If they have a flawed representative in the modern academy, it is cultural studies—which arose in the ethnological traditions that recognize differences, while succumbing to the professionalizing rules and universalizing pretenses of the modern university.

Were it not for the modern practice of naming everything under the sun, it would hardly make any difference what one calls the method Du Bois fell into without his realizing the full implications that would only become apparent once, a good century after he wrote *Souls,* the globalizing world had come to its global senses. Only in social circumstances that prevail at the turn of the twenty-first century is it possible to think of the sphere of social things as irrevocably a sphere of irreconcilable differences. Globalization's dirty trick is to call out modernity's big lie—that the world is one, thus culture is universal; hence time is forward moving, and differences are short-run flaws. With globalization, fast time forces into the open the gravity of spatial realities—the distances are easily breached, but once traversed the differences are evident. Behind Kentucky Fried Chicken in Calcutta, people beg on the streets in languages hard to follow, much less learn. Beneath the surface calm of flat similarity lie the rough underwater mountains, dark caves, and creatures man has yet to discover. The world was always this way. Only the European ideal of one cultural world led their conquerors to think otherwise. Cortez bought the program that paid for his brutal plunder in the Americas. The Aztecs he slaughtered knew better, or so one supposes. Likewise, the Queen of England must have been impressed with herself and with the imperial civilization she ruled when she welcomed Booker T. Washington to her palace. But even Mr. Washington, a master of kowtowing to whites, had to have known better. But even if in his heart of hearts he did not, Du Bois certainly did for this was the point of his politics. He, the American Negro, knew better—not because he was smarter (though Du Bois certainly most often was) but because he had the gift of second sight.

For Du Bois the gift required the dogged strength to endure the contempt, but it yielded up a considerable political lever—one that did its work most sharply in the twists and turns that are available to the cultural artist to the very extent that that they are denied to the political worker. The subtlety of Du Bois's cultural politics of difference is evident from the first in *Souls*:

> Herein lie buried many things which if read with patience may show the strange meaning of being black here in the dawning of the Twentieth Century. This meaning is not without interest to you Gentle Reader; for the problem of the Twentieth Century is the problem of the color-line. (vii)

Who exactly is the book's "Gentle Reader"? The expression, soaked in the oil of Victorian language, drips with sarcasm.

If the Gentle Reader of *Souls* can be assumed to be white (which is suggested by the allusion to "the *strange* meaning of being black"), then why no lyrics or captions under the musical scores that head each chapter? It would seem improbable that Du Bois was unwilling to offend his white readers (who in 1903 could only have been from among the white cultural elite). More likely, he sought to trick—to reveal what was hidden and to hide what was revealed. He meant to keep his side of the veil a mystery—to guard, that is, its strangeness. To stay the mystery, thus to excite the outsider, is surely one of the more effective ways to compel a reluctant and superior political and economic power. We white folks just love getting down with blacks, even when we have not a clue as to how to behave. Though some of us are some of the time, and others are all of the time, whites drawn to black experience are not necessarily fools. It can hardly be said that the European culture Du Bois admired in his own way was without merit. Were it, then Du Bois would have been the fool, which he was not. On the contrary, the genius of his literary politics is that he knew how to use the best of European culture to draw the attention of the best of its representatives. And none more in that day than Henry James, who singled out *The Souls of Black Folk* as an exemplary work of literary nonfiction. Whether his brother William, and Du Bois's friend, might have called the book to Henry's attention does not eliminate the fact that the novelist and literary critic was not easily won over for sentiment's sake.

Cultural politics take many different forms, but none so fine as the turn of a phrase to call forth both feeling and thought from the recesses of fear into the light of a different understanding. Oddly, one could also say that this, precisely, is where Du Bois's cultural work crossed over into his sociology—a vocation he accepted as much for practical as for intellectual reasons.

Though Du Bois lived well enough, his material riches were more often bestowed by others or scratched from bare bones by himself. He required a job to survive, and certainly, on the practical side, academic sociology gave him such a one in the years before 1910, when he began his twenty-five years' employment with the NAACP, and in the decade after 1935. Yet, his arrogances and affectations aside, Du Bois was never a man to work simply for money. From the earliest days, he intended to make his life's work the hard labor of being the most talented of race-men. And for this he chose to define himself as a sociologist, even while researching *The Philadelphia Negro,* when the University of Pennsylvania employed him for his fieldwork (1896–97) and hid him from public view as a teacher proper to its ticklish sense of its own excellence.

Du Bois's second book, *The Philadelphia Negro,* though ignored even today, was in fact the first serious work of urban ethnography by an American sociologist. Today, his close-in study of the Negro quarter of Philadelphia is a hard read, if only because it is so scrupulously empirical that the numbers, now archaic, would seem to render the work useless. Yet, looking more closely, *The Philadelphia Negro* is a model of solitary fieldwork in urban quarters, from which Du Bois drew attention to the rich variance of social life among several social classes, who, from the white outside, were thought to be a single and uninteresting social type meant for exclusion. The book appeared in 1899, well after Du Bois had published several of the more literary essays he later gathered for *Souls.*

If not later, one might suppose that in those last few years of the nineteenth century, he was working in two directions at once, suffering the distraction of his own two *Souls*—as an empirical sociologist, on the one hand, and as a literary man, on the other. Rather, it seems more likely that sociology, in the broad sense, was a necessary form for the expression of his cultural politics. Only a sociology can, in principle, live with actual differences. If, in the years since Du Bois started out at Atlanta University in the field, academic sociology has lapsed into its own version of modernity's culture of unifying principles, Du Bois himself used his work in the field to describe differences—and not the mere differences of continuous variations. In *Suppression of the African Slave Trade to the United States* (1896), they were the differences between the formal claims to the suppression of the trade and the bloody facts of its continuance. In *The Philadelphia Negro* (1899), they were the differences between the perceived assumptions of poverty and decadence in the Seventh Ward and the rich cultural and economic variety to be found in black urban life. In *Souls,* it was the difference between the two cultures of the Negro's souls wherein lay the space of political honesty. In *Black Reconstruction* (1935), it was the difference between the liberal belief that it was the freed people who failed themselves from 1863 until the collapse of Reconstruction in 1877 and the structural realities against which their actual achievements were heroic. A sociology is always a cultural politic also in that its work is the imagining of crosscutting differences among social things—those between the apparent and the real, those between gentle superficies and the nasty bowels of social life.

An unexpected advantage of working in resistance to the dominant order is that one is free to ignore the rules those on the other side feel they must obey in order to maintain their precious status. For Du Bois, defiance took the form of ignoring altogether the cultural distinction that many years later came to be known, by the grace of C. P. Snow, as the two cultures—the alienation of the literary arts from the various sciences. Still, this arbitrary division of mental labor had already gained ground in the last quarter of the nineteenth century as the new research universities in the United States founded themselves after the model of the German universities, where Du Bois had received much of his graduate training. The idea was to make the university less a seminary of cultural refinement and more a training ground in formal science. Du Bois knew quite well the dominant European culture's confidence in science, a confidence that hinged on keeping it separate from the arts, which, then as now, were viewed as more susceptible to "ideology," so called.

Yet, from every indication, in the work as in the life, Du Bois ignored these analytic divides and devoted his quite exquisite literary sensibilities to cultivating the ground between. To say that he believed a talented tenth of the black population was necessary unto racial uplift in the generations after Emancipation is not to say that he trusted in elites for their own sake. In point of fact, in many of his dealings, especially those at the NAACP, he ran afoul of elitist types, both white and black, precisely because they were all too ready to turn the association into a mannered society of the racially integrated. Du Bois's talented tenth was no racialized upper crust but rather a vanguard of race workers who would train and lead young men and women into qualification for social positions in which their work could turn the tables of the social order.

Souls is replete with understated outrage at those, white and black, whose elite social status crushed the young and innocent—the little white girl who refused his party card; the politicians who entered into the compromise of 1876 that destroyed Reconstruction; Booker T. Washington himself, whose policy of social separation would have led generations of freed people into lives of economic misery worse even than what they had (and often have today); the white physicians of Atlanta whose hospitals effectively doomed his little boy to death by their refusal to treat colored people; the roly-poly white Episcopal bishop who meant to limit Alexander Crummell's ministry to Black folk; and on and on. The allusions do not always drip with the sarcasm I supply, and which he would permit himself in his later writings. *Souls* is more a lament, in keeping with the Elizabethan tone of the prose. Still, Du Bois's ability to draw his own line between elites of whatever color and talented race workers can be missed only by those unwilling to read the subtext.

The Gentle Reader of *Souls* is a Victorian fiction, as was the superficial gentility of its author's prose. Du Bois knew very well that the vast majority of those who might read it would not read gently at all. Du Bois was made for the aggression required by life along the color line, and he knew how to handle himself. If he took the form of the European gentleman (a form to which he was, in fact, quite attached personally), he took it often for a political and social purpose. The man was a sociologist first and foremost, the kind of sociologist who regarded his researches as fodder for practical gains in the world as it lay before him. When, as was already happening, academic sociology joined so many other high-minded fields in seeking the high ground of a formal science, it could do this only by cutting away its original human ties with the poetry of social life. Du Bois himself could certainly drone on with all the numbers a scientist might want, as he did in his first book, his Harvard thesis, *The Suppression of the African Slave Trade,* in 1896, in *The Philadelphia Negro* three years later, and in the annual studies of rural black towns during his first tenure at Atlanta University. But, even when he worked as the empirical sociologist, Du Bois was continuously engaged in the politics and poetry of social life. In a certain sense, biographically, *Souls* in 1903 is the literary text interlinear to the hard sociology of *The Philadelphia Negro* in 1899.

But what does it mean to suggest that a book like *Souls,* with its literary finery stitched by the passionate soul of its author, is at heart a work of social theory, if not sociology outright—a politics of difference in the form of a cultural deception?

To answer any question put to Du Bois is to take an indirect path, as he intended, along the byways of his thinking, which, though plainly expressed, was never simple. This was his genius—to take the most complex of subjects and reduce them to an ostensible clarity, of which the completely brilliant synoptic history of Reconstruction, "Of the Dawn of Freedom," chapter 2, is one of the more memorable instances. In regard to this complex question of the status of his sociology amid his poetry, it is necessary to imagine the sociology of the early years of the twentieth century when Du Bois was inventing his very distinctive brand of poetic sociology as politics.

John Edgar Wideman has astutely observed[2] that 1903 was, of course, just a few years after and before two other works that changed the century to follow—Sigmund Freud's 1899 *Interpretation of Dreams* and Albert Einstein's 1905 essays that led to his general theory of relativity. Wideman's idea is that Freud, Einstein, and Du Bois, unbeknownst each to the other, were inventing new sciences that cracked the code of the apparent and superficial as they presented themselves to the naked eye.

Freud's *unconscious,* Einstein's *warped time,* and Du Bois's *doubled souls* were, in effect, each about the repressed or the unapparent modern consciousness. Some might complain that it is too much of a stretch to include the founder of post-Newtonian physics. But the point holds up if you consider the deeper substrate that links all three of them. Each was, in effect, rethinking space and time. Einstein did this most obviously by presenting the analytic evidence that time moves at different rates according to one's place in space—thus, at the far reaches of cosmic space, time does not so much lag behind as turn on itself.

Freud, of course, did not even begin to engage questions of this sort, notwithstanding his own early predilection for a kind of hydraulic model of the three parts of the psyche. But he did, in effect, require us, in time, to rethink the time of consciousness in relation to the unconscious. If the pattern of thoughts and their movements in respect to each other in the conscious mind are constantly dragging along the effects of their unconscious correlates, driven by the wish that what happens in the conscious life be always more than it is, then Freud's idea of the power of dreams is that they, too, cause the time of conscious thought to lag and, eventually (in principle at least), to collapse toward the darkness of the unthinkable.

Then, less obvious still, *The Souls of Black Folk* triangulates the more overtly scientific theories of the other two. As Wideman suggests, though a bit incompletely, *Souls* began to define for the first time the social space of the American Negro. One might say that this process had been well under way with the slave narratives, of which Fredrick Douglass's were famous the world over, and the later writings of early black feminists like Anna Julia Cooper and of Booker T. Washington himself, among many others. What distinguishes *The Souls of Black Folk,* however, is that it is very likely the first book written out of the black experience to provide a comprehensive map of the social domain of the African diaspora in America, thus making it possible to speak, however poetically, of a color line as a—perhaps even *the*—defining coordinate of the modern world.

Souls is nothing if not a compendium of essays describing the circumstances of black Americans and, through them, of black people everywhere as they were and are distributed in the global spaces. When a writer sets out to map the terra incognita of a people cut off from others, he can do this in one way and one way only—by reversing the time of social history to dig down not so much to the origins but to the archaeological layers on which the exclusions were built. This means, in effect, that to get at the depths of the excluded social life it is necessary to abandon all pretense as to the linear progress of the temporal order.

The modern world, as it was still aborning in 1903, had staked its claim on the ideal of human progress. Anyone—and this must mean *any one*—with experience on the other side of the color line, among other lines of exclusion, knows very well that progress is a fraud, taking the form of quackery. Rub this promise of a better future on your wounds and you will feel better soon—where the "soon" was never soon enough, certainly not a soon to come before the daybreak when the quack had already moved his cart to the next town. For Du Bois, to challenge the modern moral theory of time as progress was to redraw the map of the whole social domain, which could not thereafter be less than a global domain. The social could no longer be a world thought to be rising in a westward direction to a higher place—"purple mountains' majesty above the fruited plains," that sort of thing. The social domain, rather, would have to be drawn as one that, whatever heights might be attainable, led the pilgrim first into the pits of social despair. Du Bois's own theoretical and practical reversal of historical time was not fully developed until *Black Reconstruction* in 1935. But one can find it clearly in *Souls* in 1903—most strikingly in the two-*Souls* figure of the American Negro condemned to contempt, seeing himself as others see him, warring against this inner self imposed by the judgments of others, yet carrying on with the gift of second sight.

> [T]he Negro is a sort of seventh son, born with a veil, and gifted with second-sight in this American world,—a world which yields him no true self-consciousness, but only lets him see himself through the revelation of the other world. It is a peculiar sensation, this double consciousness, this sense of always looking at one's self through the eyes of others, of measuring one's soul by the tape of a world that looks on in amused contempt and pity. One ever feels his twoness,—an American, a Negro; two *Souls*, two thoughts, two unreconciled strivings; two warring ideals in one dark body, whose dogged strength alone keeps it from being torn asunder.[3]

This, the most famous of all lines in the book, sets the tone for the laments that run through the book as a whole, but the lamentations are always glossed, as here, by the gift of second sight—the power that comes to those who, while held in contempt, exploit the shadows to see the world more deeply. The veil, like the color line, is a poetic figure, but it conveys a strong theoretical principle, one that is close by those of Freud and Einstein. If you reverse the naive time of social progress, you will discover the hidden social spaces on the other side of the line. Within these spaces mysteries are held—mysteries not unique to those there relegated, but general to the whole of a world that allows, against its own professed ideals, such a space to stand as it does against the self-conscious pretense of the Good Society.

Hence, the rhizomatic connection to Freud and Einstein, a sketch—if not a robust social theory of modern realities—of realities that were, in the first five or so years of the twentieth century, already being reconsidered with respect to the interior space of the psyche and to the far exterior space of the universe. What Du Bois did in *Souls* was to write the general theory of social relativity by interpreting the dream of the modern world—and nowhere more painfully than in the book's fourth essay, "Of the Meaning of Progress." Inasmuch as his great European sociological contemporaries, Emile Durkheim and Max Weber, were doing something quite similar at about the same time, it is not the stretch it may seem to say that, among them, Du Bois was the poetic sociologist who wrote in the metaphoric language that was required to utter the harsh truths the others were aware of but could not quite believe.

As it happens, two key texts by Du Bois's European contemporaries reflected, if not quite as overtly, just the same readiness to contend with the social meanings of time in Western places. One of them was, oddly, related to *Souls.* That one was Max Weber's *The Protestant Ethic and the Spirit of Capitalism,* which, like *Souls,* was cobbled together out of essays. Weber had emerged from his long depression to write in 1904–5 a series of essays on the question of the social origins of capitalism. In this period he made his famous visit to the United States, which included a visit with Du Bois in Atlanta the summer of 1904. Weber offered to broker a German translation of *Souls,* which he much admired. It is likely that Weber's American visit that summer sealed his conviction as to the central theme of *Protestant Ethic*—that capitalism arose first as an ethical spirit that was nowhere more apparent in that day than in the United States. Surely, Weber had seen or heard of Du Bois's studies of the hard-working blacks of the rural South, which were in fact the occasion for the summer conferences that drew Weber to Atlanta. How, if at all, those studies influenced Weber is hard to say, but certainly the disciplined work ethic he saw in Du Bois the man did not discourage the idea.

It is tricky business to suggest that in *Protestant Ethic* Weber was exploring the same sort of rethinking of social time as Du Bois and the others were—save for one thing. The Weber thesis makes no sense, really, if one does not see that it is about social time. The spirit of capitalism that Weber attributed to the calculating religious ethic of sixteenth-century Calvinism was, he thought, an emergent revolutionary attitude toward practical time. Where traditionalism, the ethic modernism had to overcome, was oriented, in Weber's magnificent phrase, to the "eternal yesterday," the modern spirit of the capitalist entrepreneur was future oriented. The distinction between traditional-as-past and modern-as-future is so commonplace today that we forget what Weber did not: that the revolution that gave rise (if Weber is correct) to the modern world was a revolution in the way men and women think of social time. In a certain sense, for there to be entrepreneurs, there must be an ethic that legitimates a strictly future-oriented practical attitude in the affairs of daily life. Such an ethic had to have been invented, which is what Weber argues the Calvinists did, entirely by accident. They wanted men to attend to the eternal. What they got was this-worldly asceticism, which amounts to calculating everything according to its future value.

In 1903, the same year that *Souls* appeared, Emile Durkheim, with his nephew Marcel Mauss, published *Primitive Classification*—the book that would grow into Durkheim's masterwork of 1912, *Elementary Forms of the Religious Life.* The latter book is deceptively named in that religion, given Durkheim's idea of it as the moral foundation of social life, is only the beginning of its story. *Elementary Forms* turned out to be, in effect, a thesis on the social foundations of time, space, and the other categories of mental life. This thesis was already present, full-blown, in his 1903 book with Mauss. What were these *Primitive Classifications*? Precisely those mental categories of time, space, causality, and totality that, since the Greeks, have been considered essential to thinking itself. In other words, even Durkheim—and no one of that era was more the self-conscious academic sociologist—was preoccupied with questions of the importance of the theories of social time and space to sociology.

It may seem odd in the extreme to suggest that *Primitive Classifications* is a book of the same order as *Protestant Ethic,* much less *Souls, Interpretation of Dreams,* or Einstein's early essays. But, on reconsideration, Weber and Durkheim in their books of 1903 to 1905—though dealing with quite different subjects—were contending with much the same problem, which in turn was the problem the others, including Du Bois, had also to face.

This was the dilemma facing all serious social theorists at the turn of that century. Though none of them could have known when the Great War of 1914 would come, anyone in and about Europe had to have realized that there was deep trouble brewing in the innocent world of modern progress. Weber wrote of the out-of-control effects of modern social organization, of the bureaucratic machine. Durkheim, in his earlier works, wrote of the anomic nature of modern industrial societies rife with class conflict. In a fashion, both of them sought a way around or beyond Marx's critique that modern capitalist societies, far from being the harbingers of new social progress, were every bit as dehumanizing as those that came before. Alienation, or estrangement, from one's productive labor is no more than a superficially benign version of the evils of the slave and despotic modes of production.

For any serious social thinker of the time to have deciphered clues as to the dark side of the modern order, it would have been necessary to be alert to the harsh realities of modern hope. Though none of these more sociological thinkers did this as straightforwardly as Freud, all were keenly aware that any sort of socially responsible method for thinking about social things at the turn of that century had to account for the inscrutability of meaning. To not be willing to take empirical things at face value is, thereby, to explore new ways of examining the hidden meanings behind surface appearances, which is exactly what all the great thinkers of that day were doing. And Du Bois in *Souls* was no exception.

Though, in the first years of the twentieth century, the moral question was differently put than in the first years of the twenty-first, it amounted to much the same as today. *How are we to get by in these times?* It was a question that only on the surface appeared to be a bitter complaint. In fact, it was a question of moment and one that required those who would answer it to treat the times in a perfectly serious manner. Though it is clearer today when global speed has meant the relations of time to space are at least unstable, if not fluid, in a century earlier the question of how one deals with changes so rapid that the worlds seem to be lost is one requiring a rethinking of the social basis of time and social space. *Souls* did this by mapping the social terrain of the African diaspora to America, which in turn required a suspension of faith in the smooth forward flow of historical time. In this regard, Du Bois was no different from the other sociologists of his day, Weber and Durkheim, or from the full company of others, from the microanalyst Freud to the macro-physicist Einstein.

Perhaps it is so that whenever social changes occur with shocking speed those subjected to the transformations and loss of it all are forced to think deeply about the underlying causes of social things, including the social foundations of history, time, and space. If it is true today, then it was just as true in the first years of the previous century just before the crisis of the war of 1914. But, after the Great War, from 1920 on, for a good five decades until the world revolutions of 1968, the dominant forms of practical sociology and cultural politics largely (if not entirely) ignored the social skepticism of the founding generation in which Du Bois deserves to be mentioned. Strangely enough, Du Bois and writers of his inclinations were not rediscovered until such time as social things became sufficiently unglued. It is not that this reawakening that came about in the last quarter of the century was caused by Du Bois or instigated by *Souls* and other such works. But, certainly, the theory of cultural and social relativity found in *Souls* might be a symptom of those earlier times, which was lost and then found in the century that ensued.

As he claimed in "The Forethought" to *Souls,* Du Bois meant "to show the strange meaning of being black here at the dawning of the Twentieth Century."[4] These meanings were strange, even a century later, precisely because they could be conveyed, for the most part, only by the authority of experience—"being black here," that is, in this time and place. Thus, the forethought in which he draws up the color line as the decisive vector of global politics is also a crypto-social physics—a shadowy sketch, visible to those in the know, of a given social space in time certain. The time of the Negro soul is always out of sync with the glacial time of European progress. Whether Du Bois's Gentle Reader was white or black, or both, is left for the reader to decide. To read this book one must decide whether to follow him to the mysterious places or, if already there, to trust him when he maps them for all the white world to see, if only they would.

Souls then launches immediately into the experience. "Of Our Spiritual Strivings," the first and most famous chapter containing the double-consciousness idea, begins with an experience so universal that even the Gentle White Readers will be brought up short: "Between me and the other world there is ever an unasked question: unasked by some through feelings of delicacy; by others through the difficulty of rightly framing it. All, nevertheless, flutter round it. They approach me in a half-hesitant sort of way, eye me curiously or compassionately, and then, instead of saying directly, How does it feel to be a problem? they say, I know an excellent colored man in my town. . . ."[5] Could there be a cleverer way to put the alleged Gentle Reader in his position? Whether white or not, hardly anywhere in racially divided experience (which is virtually everywhere in the world as it was then, is now, and will be for time to come), one is brought up short. The Gentle Author to the Gentle Reader is playing honest with the experience that all have heard of or had.

"How does it feel to be a problem?" The unasked question seals the method. The problem must be the problem of the twentieth century—the problem of the color line. He, the Negro intellectual, the uninvited spokesman of an impossible cultural situation, puts himself, in the subtext, and the American Negro, in the text, as the one whom any Gentle Reader, from wherever along the color line, must trust if she is to read on. For the whites it was, especially then, a strange experience to follow an author who was, in principle, unreal. Booker T. Washington, whatever his virtues, whites could trust, given his pledge not to seek social partnership. But a Negro intellectual, like this author, was another matter, as still he is. Du Bois, thus, begins with a simple little story of an experience his reader surely has had. It is offered as his personal experience, but Du Bois himself is little more than the token of the trope. The color-line trope, delicately applied to protect the sensibilities of the reader, saves the allusion from the ruin of *mere* subjective experience. This is the method of the standpoint—not personal but social in its embrace, not local but global in its reach.

"Of Our Spiritual Strivings" then turns to his childhood and the injury inflicted (but denied) by the little white girl who refused his party card "peremptorily, with a glance." In this one gesture the force of the veil of race reality comes into view. "Then it dawned upon me with a certain suddenness that I was different from the others; or like, mayhap, in heart and life and longing, but shut out from their world by a vast veil."[6]

After which comes the memorable passage of the "twoness" theme: "After the Egyptian and Indian, the Greek and Roman, the Teuton and Mongolian, the Negro is a sort of seventh son, born with a veil, and gifted with second-sight in this American world, a world which yields him no true self-consciousness, but only lets him see himself through the revelation of the other world." The weight of the two-*Souls* theme is on the American Negro, but the volume of it is the global history of the races. The rest of the book flows from this, in a more systematic way than might be expected for a collection of essays.

The reader, gentle or not, would do well to think of the first four chapters of *The Souls of Black Folk* as at least the outlines of a manifesto of Du Bois's thinking, including his method. As the first chapter establishes the sociology of the two-souled American Negro, the second, "Of the Dawn of Freedom," picks up the trope of the color line to tell the story of the rise and fall of Reconstruction in the post–Civil War South. This would be the theme to which Du Bois would return more than thirty years later in *Black Reconstruction*, which, after *The Philadelphia Negro,* is his most explicit work of sociology, in the more familiar academic sense, and very probably the greatest of all his works. For whites of the North and South, the Civil War remains the dividing line of American history. For blacks, the short time of Reconstruction (1861–76) was a gestation period that eventually renewed the color line with ever more ferocity. After a period of social progress facilitated by the Freedmen's Bureau and other northern agencies (private as well as public), hope was obliterated by the Compromise of 1876, which turned the South back over to the heirs of the former planters and, in quick order, to Jim Crow, which grew at first by local terror, only officially sanctioned in 1896 when the United States Supreme Court (in *Plessy v. Ferguson*) blessed the already deep racial divisions—separate but unequal.[7]

"Of Mr. Booker T. Washington and Others," chapter 3, would seem at first look to break the gathering pattern of the book, but for one thing: Du Bois's two cultural souls—the one scientific, the other literary—allowed him the free play to set his cultural work and his sociology to political purposes. Booker T. Washington, being the race-man in the days after the death of Frederick Douglass in 1895 and before the rise of Du Bois himself in 1910, was the necessary subject to which a book of 1903 had to turn after setting out the standpoint experience and defining its conditions in the history of Reconstruction and its aftermath. Du Bois's famous challenge to the principal of Tuskegee was not *mere* ambition. In fact, the essay is respectful in every way, more so, one might say, than the tone with which he has already caught up the Gentle White Reader of the book. Booker T. Washington, his senior by a good dozen years and many degrees of social recognition, was very much more than a rival for influence. Washington's philosophy of accommodation with the restored planter class in the South served, in effect (if not intention), to reinforce the color line. Washington's famous Atlanta Compromise speech was delivered barely a year after the death of Douglass—separate in all things social, one in matters of common progress. He had delivered to the whites, North and South, just what they demanded: assent by the most prominent American Negro in the land to their policy of racial separation—separate, but unequal.

Du Bois could not have become who and what he became had he remained silent on this question.

"Of Mr. Booker T. Washington" is usually interpreted as a first statement of Du Bois's talented tenth strategy, which he describes in so many words three chapters later in "Of the Training of Black Men." The strategy was just that, of course—and was one that would necessarily appeal to a man of such learning and scholarly accomplishments as Du Bois. But, again, it was not just a self-aggrandizing policy. While it is true that a man like Du Bois could hardly have been expected to join ranks with Washington's industrial education compromise, his affirmation of the urgency of higher education for the most talented black men and women was founded in his own deeply felt experience in the South.

It could hardly have been by chance that Du Bois, always keen to the moves he made, followed his all-too-gentle excoriation of Mr. Booker T. Washington with the tragic tale of Josie—"Of the Meaning of Progress," chapter 4 and the coda of the four-chapter manifesto of *Souls*. "How shall man measure Progress there where the dark-faced Josie lies?" How indeed! "Of the Meaning of Progress" is the attenuation of the rebuke of Booker T. Washington. Why must we be against compromise with the liberal powers that turned the South over to Jim Crow? Because of Josie, who becomes the emblem of the false promise of liberal progress. Du Bois was not against industrial education, or working people, any more than he was an elitist in any respect other than in personal style. Josie's lost life and early death taught the truth of black impoverishment and the falsity of American culture. He must have seen her face in the bright young students he taught at Atlanta University—the ones who escaped the hills for a reasonable hope of a better life.

Thereafter follow the six chapters of *Souls* that could very aptly be described as the social map of the Negro South. "Of the Wings of Atalanta" turns on the irony of using Atalanta, the Greek maiden of legend who lost her virgin beauty to her own greed, as a figure for Atlanta, the Queen of the Cotton Kingdom and the city in which he passed a good bit of his adult life. By setting the territorial coordinates of the Cotton Kingdom, he is able then to return to the talented tenth strategy in "Of the Training of Black Men," where he ties the knot between a political theory of racial uplift and the social realities measured by Josie. Then, in chapters 7 and 8, comes the social map. "Of the Black Belt" and "Of the Quest of the Golden Fleece" describe in concrete terms the facts and effects of the restoration of the economics, if not the culture, of the plantation system.

Though "Of the Black Belt" and "Of the Quest of the Golden Fleece" were originally published together (in 1901 in *The World's Work*) and tell the story of the racial economics of the postwar South, they are set in quite different languages. The former is very much more a descriptive human geography of the Black Belt from Atlanta south through Georgia to Dougherty County—at the heart of the Cotton Kingdom and one of the counties most heavily populated by rural blacks forced to work as peasants in the restored plantation system. The latter is more literary, from the figure of cotton as the golden fleece of this sordid kingdom to the richly narrative accounts of families. As the previous chapter maps the descent into the Black Belt from Atlanta south to Dougherty County, chapter 8 is a travel narrative through the county where the suffering all along the belt is most acute.

The next two chapters of the social map section revert to the two dominant social themes likely to be on the minds of Du Bois's Gentle Readers. Chapter 9, "Of the Sons of Master and Man," is the most straightforwardly formal of all the selections, owing no doubt to its first publication in 1901 in the *Annals of the American Academy of Political and Social Sciences*. Still, it deals directly with the social history of what would soon be called in the academy "race relations"—the subject of Washington's compromise in 1896, and the subject on the minds of everyone white, South and North. The Civil War meant different things to whites and blacks, but to both it meant a terrifying bloodbath fought over social differences that turned on racial differences. The chapter following, "Of the Faith of the Fathers," is one of the fairest descriptions of the black church as a social institution that one could imagine, given the author's native indifference to primitive, emotional religious expression. This essay takes up one of the monuments of the social map—the one powerful institution that defined the culture and pride of the American Negro more than any other.

It is true, of course, that *Souls* remains a collection of essays composed over a wide range of subjects. Yet, when the parts are read looking for the whole, Du Bois's cultural politics are clear. The composition of a book out of separate essays is itself an art, all the more so when the book serves, in effect, as an announcement of its author's life work. Naturally, some would suggest that to credit Du Bois with so clear a sense of purpose is to romanticize too much. Yet, the record could not be clearer that this Negro intellectual, from a young age, meant to be what he had become. That a man who took so fast to academic work would follow the publications of two very academic works with a book like *Souls* is hard to dismiss. Even were it done, the skeptic would have to contend with the impossible-to-dismiss evidence that the contents of the essays in *Souls,* when read as a whole, are anything but random—and anything but out of line with the life and work that followed. Thus, in my view, even the last four essays of the book, easily those least well integrated with the rest, served their literary and political purposes. *Souls* ends by coming back to the beginning—to the manifesto of the first four chapters and the social map of the Black Belt in the next six. Then comes "Of the Passing of the First-Born," the account of the death of Du Bois's firstborn son, Burghardt, in Atlanta. Having myself lost a child and written about the experience, I know that there are no more dangerous literary waters than those stirred by one's own lingering pain and the terrible distance it keeps from the experiences of those for whom one writes.

> He died at eventide, when the sun lay like a brooding sorrow above the western hills, veiling its face; when the winds spoke not, and the trees, the great green trees he loved, stood motionless. I saw his breath beat quicker and quicker, pause, and then his little soul leapt like a star that travels in the night and left a world of darkness in its train. The day changed not; the same tall trees peeped in at the windows, the same green grass glinted in the setting sun. Only in the chamber of death writhed the world's most piteous thing—a childless mother.[8]

Burghardt's death, it hardly need be said, was even more agonizing than Josie's. Still, Du Bois manages to shift the story away from himself—to the child, to the mother, and, in the end of the short essay, to the color line.

The cry of despair at the death of a child is a fragile thread to Josie's death and all the others along the color line and the Black Belt. "Of Alexander Crummell" (1819–98) is a tribute to the spiritual father of the talented tenth idea. Of all the race-men who preceded him, Crummell was the one who, like Du Bois himself, always had Africa well in mind. (Crummell spent more than a decade in Liberia.) Then follows the one piece of fiction in the collection. "Of the Coming of John" is certainly more than a bit overdrawn as fiction goes. Yet, the story is very likely an allegory based on Du Bois's experiences. Two boys, black and white, are playmates in a small weary town of the

South. Both are named John. They grow to manhood and leave for college—the white to Princeton, with all it offered the white gentlemen of the South; the black to a college in Pennsylvania, where he nearly fails before pulling himself together. Back home, the black John's return from an exceptional education is eagerly awaited. Studies over, he returns to much excitement. But he can no longer share in the ways of those he left behind. His worldly training leaves him cold to their traditional ways. Outside the circle of his black community, John encounters the white John, also returned from college, who knows him not and treats him with the disdain men of his race reserve for those of John's. In cool rage, John murders the white John, caught raping a dark sister. John returns home, to sit and await his fate. The story ends before the lynch mob arrives.

The book concludes with "Of the Sorrow Songs," which would be an afterthought of sorts were it not that this essay decodes the hitherto understated two-cultures theme that lends force to the book's cultural politics. The songs, which mark each of the essays in *Souls,* remind one of the mystery of the years, of the terrible sadness that wrought the magnificent warring souls of the American Negro. "Of the Coming of John" is perhaps a cautionary tale of the troubles that lie ahead for the talented who return to the source of their experience. The "Sorrow Songs" point the reader back to slavery, the middle passage, Africa. The tale of John points him ahead to the uncertain future men and women of John's experience can have at a risk.

Du Bois consistently turned his rage into the hard work of a literary, sociological, and political life. He never failed in school, never slew the oppressor. Still, he did not eschew the rage, which more often than not came forth as righteous indignation directed equally at the black inheritors of Washington's compromise and the white elite of Princetonian manners.

The Souls of Black Folk is now in the hands of new generations of readers—more of them honestly gentle to its themes than Du Bois could have anticipated. If some now read the book for instruction as to the mysteries of the veil—as a cultural text—and others read it as a resource to pick up the struggle its author carried forth—as a political text—then both are the rightful heirs of Du Bois's work.

It is often said that Du Bois, the man and his writings, were the source of the most prominent of the Negro intellectuals who followed him, none more than Frantz Fanon. *Black Skin/White Masks* (1952) was indeed a kind of double-consciousness account of the violence of the colonial world. But Fanon, writing amid the violence of the decolonizing struggles in Africa, saw the Negro intellectual as one who had no choice but to enter the violence imposed by the colonizer: "Each native who goes back over the line is a radical condemnation of the methods and of the regime; and the native intellectual finds in the scandal he gives rise to a justification and an encouragement to persevere in the path he has chosen."[9] Though most seriously a man trained in European culture, Fanon, the Negro intellectual, was much more the direct agent of political action and much less willing, for his own reasons, to keep the tensions that were central to Du Bois's method.

At the other extreme, today's Negro intellectuals are very often rebuked by those who presume to understand race politics for having gone too far on the cultural side. And none more so than Cornel West:

> The new cultural politics of difference are neither simply oppositional in contesting the mainstream (or *male*stream) for inclusion, nor transgressive in the avant-garde sense of shocking conventional bourgeois audiences. Rather they are distinct articulations of talented (and usually privileged) contributors to culture who desire to align themselves with demoralized, demobilized, depoliticized and disorganized people in order to empower and enable social action and, if possible, to enlist collective insurgency for the expansion of freedom, democracy, and individuality.[10]

Even those who don't quite get West's artistic work in cinema and hip-hop music can grant that he is doing something right when the art so upsets a president of Harvard University—and especially so when every now and again one learns that he preached not long ago at an African American church out of the urban ways.

Whether the Negro intellectual is able, as West says and Du Bois said, to "align" himself with the dispossessed, to serve even as their representative in spite of the crisis of representation, will remain a question as old as the ages.

What is beyond question is that West, like Fanon, like Du Bois—their differences aside—understood that the role of the Negro intellectual was to stand amid the conflicting social differences—both in the community and in the world. Harold Cruse as well as anyone has put the crisis of the Negro intellectual's political work as a crisis less of representation of the Negro experience to the white world than a crisis within the Negro soul over the seriousness of its cultural politics, including the intellectual's responsibility to confront the black bourgeoisie that, especially now, many decades after Cruse wrote in 1967, colludes with the white world to degrade the Negro artist:

> The Negro creative intellectuals cannot exert themselves to deal with the roots of these problems, because they permit too many of the surface issues to pass without dealing with *them*. The question of Ellington and [the denial of] the Pulitzer Prize is a surface issue. The prize itself is not really that important, but what lies behind the denial of the prize *is*: a whole history of organized duplicity and exploitation of the Negro jazz artist—the complicated tie-in between booking agencies, the musicians' unions, the recording companies, the music publishers, the managers, the agents, the theater owners, the nightclub owners, the crooks, shysters, and racketeers.[11]

Are the shysters all white? In a world that knows men like Don King we know not.

The crisis of the Negro intellectual is a crisis of cultural politics, but it is not simply or solely about race. This Du Bois very well understood, especially in the later years when, after 1940, he gradually gave up on America to become more and more the global figure. He died in Africa a Ghanaian citizen in 1963, the year when *The Wretched of the Earth* was published, two years after the early death of its author, who, like Du Bois, left the Americas for Africa. Perhaps had Du Bois worked for years among the miserable who were confined to a mental hospital in Algiers, as had Fanon, then he might have come to Africa sooner, there to join the suffering.

This, of course, is the question put, since it was put by Marx, to the intellectual—what exactly is the intellectual's relation to those for whom she dares to speak? "Intellectuals from subjugated groups continually confront the literal and metaphorical option of dropping the pen and picking up the gun."[12] Does the intellectual have the right to pursue art for art's sake, thus to forsake the community experience from which he takes his artistic material? Does the community have the right to demand of its intellectuals that they set aside, even for a time, their art to experience the suffering? It is certainly true that Du Bois did not resolve, or address, these questions as they would later be addressed—or, better put, as they would later force themselves on Negro intellectuals and artists.

More than anyone writing today, Jerry Gafio Watts has described the traps and possibilities of the community in the life and mind of the Negro intellectual. On the one hand, she must struggle with the temptation to give in to the victim status. On the other, however, the Negro intellectual is traditionally in a socially marginal position, thus denied access to the white-controlled resources for artistic production and performance and reception. Yet, Watts nicely describes the position as a "betwixt and between" that leaves open the advantages it provides. Thus, on the other hand, confinement to the excluded community requires but also provides an "intellectual space"—from which to do and deepen the work. Referring to Amiri Baraka, Watts says: "The conundrum confronting Baraka was to develop a political and intellectual worldview that would simultaneously facilitate tactical political and social thinking, authorize but discipline the articulation of black rage, mediate his erratic feelings of estrangement from Black America, nurture the psychic space necessary for him to realize his creative, artistic talents."[13] Without insisting that Baraka is the final model of the Negro intellectual, Watts's portrayal of him, and through him the type itself, captures the tensions of the betwixt and between of the cultural politics of differences.

It has been a long journey from Du Bois and *Souls,* through Fanon, then Cruse, to Baraka, West, and Watts, not excluding the countless others who today come before the white world as, in Du Bois's day, they could not. Du Bois's cultural politics were not as willingly violent as were Fanon's, nor as sociologically attuned to the economic realities as were Cruse's, nor as revolutionary as Baraka's, not even as publicly scandalous as West's. Yet, if he set the course, he set it by taking it upon himself and thereby setting himself up as a token, if not a model, of the Negro intellectual. By today's standards his cultural work may seem mild mannered. But when measured against the times, it was well suited to the conditions under which he worked and changed. He was, in respect to those times, every bit the revolutionary as were those who followed.

> The black man has functioned in the white man's world as a fixed star, as an immovable pillar; and as he moves out of his place, heaven and earth are shaken to their foundations.
> —*James Baldwin, "My Dungeon Shook"*

5

The Souls of Black Folk *and* *Afro-American Intellectual Life*

Jerry G. Watts

Too many contemporary students of American intellectual life consume and rehash commodified clippings of Du Boisian ideas rather than actually engage his substantive thought. Du Boisian ideas, particularly those associated with *The Souls of Black Folk,* too often function as quotable markers of an exposure to an Afro-American intellectual tradition. How often have we heard tidbits of Du Bois restated as if they constitute Rosetta stones of black intellectual inquiry? Three frequently recited Du Boisian snippets immediately come to mind:

> "How does it feel to be a problem?"
> "One ever feels his two-ness, an American, a Negro; two souls, two thoughts, two unreconciled strivings; two warring ideals in one dark body."
> "The problem of the twentieth century is the problem of the color line."

Three quotes do not capture the meanings of *The Souls of Black Folk.* One book, even one as momentous as *The Souls of Black Folk,* does not constitute sufficient grounds to assess the entirety of Du Bois's corpus. And Du Bois, however Promethean a figure, does not, by himself, constitute an Afro-American intellectual tradition.

Though the stature of Du Bois has risen drastically within white American academic circles during the past forty years, it remains unclear whether he has become accepted as an appendage or if his writings are considered foundational when reevaluating twentieth-century American thought.

I admit to having been stunned when in 1987 I first read Russell Jacoby's *The Last Intellectuals: American Culture in the Age of Academe*.[1] Jacoby laments the decline of the public intellectual during the latter quarter of the twentieth century. He is troubled by the dominance of universities as the home of intellectuals at the expense of independent journals and so forth. In addition, Jacoby is distressed because he does not see younger generations of intellectuals emerging as replacements for aging (and dying) public intellectual figures like Daniel Bell, Lionel Trilling, Irving Howe, and John Kenneth Galbraith.

I had no qualms with many of the thrusts of his argument but nowhere in Jacoby's book is there any hint that Afro-American intellectuals might exist.[2] This erasure of black thinkers leads to distortions in his argument. For instance, James Baldwin was undoubtedly one of the most significant public intellectual figures of the 1960s. He certainly reached audiences far beyond those reached collectively by Howe, Bell, and Trilling. And who in the twentieth century was a greater embodiment of public intellectual engagement than W. E. B. Du Bois? Du Bois might be twentieth-century America's ideal public intellectual. What's more, he regularly reached a more diverse public audience than the audiences reached by Howe, Bell, and Trilling. Clearly, Jacoby's book is a case of racial parochialism or racist parochialism. What made Jacoby's parochialism even more stunning was that he was a significant figure in the American intellectual Left.[3] The marginalization of black intellectuals in books purporting to be about American intellectuals still occurs regularly.[4] Nevertheless, I suspect that it occurs less frequently today than it did twenty years ago and that it occurred twenty years ago less frequently than it occurred fifty years ago.

One hundred years ago it would have been ludicrous to deliver a lecture before most academic audiences in America on the topic of Afro-American social and political philosophy. Except perhaps for the few Afro-American learned societies and reading groups, most American audiences would have considered the idea of Afro-American social thought an oxymoron.[5] Negroes were deemed to have emotions and even opinions, but it would have been laughable to suggest that they could produce a coherent social philosophy. The pervasiveness of antiblack cultural racism buttressed by scientific substantiation of black genetic/biological inferiority minimized the possibility of envisioning an Afro-American as a serious thinker. Nevertheless, some early twentieth-century Afro-Americans not only imagined themselves as vital thinkers but, in fact, were formidable intellects.

In 1898, one formidable Afro-American intellect, Alexander Crummell, delivered a lecture before the American Negro Academy titled "The Attitude of the American Mind Toward the Negro Intellect."[6] In that lecture, Crummell criticized white racist hostility to the cultivation of black creative genius. He concluded that given white hostility, blacks would have to create their own institutions for intellectual nurturance. In his study of twentieth-century Afro-American intellectuals, Ross Posnock convincingly argued that despite their marginalization at the hands of white racism, Alexander Crummell and W. E. B. Du Bois were among the first authentically cosmopolitan thinkers to emerge in twentieth-century America.[7] According to Posnock, Du Bois and his black confreres constituted the initial cadre of modern American intellectuals.[8]

Posnock's reconsideration of early twentieth-century Afro-American intellectuals as cosmopolitans offers an important corrective to racially parochial commentaries on American intellectual history. However, his understanding of cosmopolitanism is flawed insofar as it elides a serious interrogation of the centrality of sexism in the lives and thought of these cosmopolitan, male Afro-American intellectuals. Crummell, Du Bois, and the other members of the male-only American Negro Academy could only be considered cosmopolitan if their sexism is ignored.[9] Posnock ignores their conception of the authentic Negro intellectual as necessarily male.[10]

We no longer live in an America that instinctively dismisses the idea of an Afro-American philosopher or serious thinker. Nor, for that matter, must the Afro-American serious thinker be male. Nonetheless, the contemporary image of the Afro-American intellectual remains more entrenched in America's cultural margins than those popular images of Afro-Americans as parole violators; welfare queens; athletes; entertainers; and hand-waving, spirit-filled, gyrating Holy Ghost Christians. I suspect that most Americans, black and white, are more at ease with images of blacks as high-flying dunk "artists" and stand-up comics than as commentators on American foreign policy, critics of nuclear energy, or federal judges.[11] Certainly, there have been exceptions to this pattern. From 2000 to 2004, Colin Powell served as secretary of state, a position heretofore reserved for whites. Perhaps even more pathbreaking has been the presence of a black woman, Condoleezza Rice, as President George W. Bush's national security advisor and, later, secretary of state. Intriguingly, Afro-Americans may experience greater cultural acceptance within the political sphere than within the realm of publicly acknowledged intellects.

The dominant images associated with contemporary black Americans may help to explain, among other things, the paucity of black political commentators on national television. In being certified by national media organizations, such commentators are granted cultural authority to explain and/or legitimate American political behavior. The conspicuous absence of analytical sophistication on the part of media-anointed white gurus such as Chris Mathews, Fred Barnes, Morton Kondracke, Dan Rather, Brit Hume, Tom Brokaw, Bill O'Reilly, Tucker Carlson, Michael Barone, Dick Morris, Mark Shields, and William Kristol precludes the suggestion that the absence of blacks in such positions stems from their failure to meritocratically earn their public voices. Not only is the absence of blacks in "analytical" media positions obvious, it is equally obvious that the general American public does not perceive the absence of black commentators on television as problematic or even as an absence.[12]

If present-day American society remains racially parochial in its imaging of Afro-Americans,[13] consider the images of blacks that saturated American society a hundred years ago. The pathological white, antiblack racism that was hegemonic at that time precluded, for most white Americans, the possible existence of a serious black thinker and, even more so, a black American who claimed to be a "man-of-culture."[14] The W. E. B. Du Bois who burst onto the American intellectual scene at the end of the nineteenth century must have been considered a racial freak in the eyes of many whites.[15] Du Bois was a racial abnormality not only because he was so different from the "everyday Negro" but also because he was so unlike the normalized imagined possibilities of Afro-American existence. The overwhelming majority of Negro contemporaries of the young Du Bois were illiterate and imprisoned in peasantlike, neoslave existences in the rural South. Of those blacks who lived in the North, most were barely educated urban dwellers who resided in overcrowded ghettos that were the precursors of the twentieth-century urban slums. Northern black workers were overwhelmingly confined to low-skilled labor sectors. For instance, in 1900, 76 percent of Afro-Americans in Philadelphia worked in either unskilled labor or domestic and personal service jobs.[16] Along with poverty, predominantly black urban areas in northern cities were riddled with crime, vice, and violence.[17]

Amidst white racist domination and black economic impoverishment and criminality, there arose a small segment of urban Negroes who were economically and socially of a higher status than the vast majority of blacks. This emerging "better element" of blacks consisted of those few who had broken through exclusionary racial barriers to obtain stable manufacturing jobs; those who owned small businesses and retail stores such as barbershops and cleaning services; morticians; real estate property owners/renters; a small number of educated professionals such as schoolteachers, doctors, and lawyers; and a small ministerial sector of seminary-trained, formal orators.[18]

Though economically on a higher level than most blacks, the "better element of Negroes" was not, generally speaking, on equal economic footing with the stable white working class. Yet, at this early moment in Afro-American urban class formation, significant elements within the black nonpoor began to aspire to and vicariously attain an intraethnic social status as "ethnic elites." In effect, nonpoor blacks were able to attain an intraethnic, elite self-definition despite the fact that they were not economically on a par with the white elites or even the white middle class. The black elite came to be defined by stable employment, social etiquette, Christian values, restrained sexuality, and repressed emotionalism rather than income or wealth. As Kevin Gaines has shown, this "better element of Negroes" championed not only ethnic self-help but service to the black masses. Because of their superior cultural values (more like those of whites than those of most blacks), it was their self-acknowledged duty to "uplift the race."[19]

Despite the status pretensions among the better element of Negroes, at the end of the nineteenth century there were only a few blacks like Du Bois who had attained formal academic training or other professional pedigrees that were on a par with those of high-status white academics or professionals. Most blacks who had obtained a higher education had done so via black educational institutions, which for the most part were not the equal of better private white colleges. For instance, few black ministers, including those in major black pulpits, had obtained degrees from elite, predominantly white seminaries. An exception was Francis Grimke, who ministered to the "better element" Negroes as pastor of the Fifteenth Street Presbyterian Church in Washington, D.C. Grimke had graduated from Princeton Theological Seminary in 1878.[20] Another professional exception was his brother, Archibald Grimke, a lawyer in Boston who had graduated from Harvard Law School in 1874.[21]

At the end of the nineteenth century, the prevailing socialization among Negroes, even those who had educational pedigrees similar to those of their white peers, was to accept the reality that their professional lives would be constrained by the color line. Though he had attended Harvard for his undergraduate and graduate education and had studied in Germany, Du Bois had been socialized to repress whatever lingering ambitions he might have entertained of teaching at Harvard or even lesser predominantly white colleges such as a Boston University or an Amherst College. In effect, during the first half of the twentieth century, Du Bois and those relatively few blacks who had obtained elite graduate education were forced to live bifurcated lives. They could share the intellectual ambitions of their white graduate school peers and professors but they could not share their academic ambitions.

During the first half of the twentieth century, Howard University was able to attract a faculty of elite educated blacks that rivaled or surpassed the faculties at many predominantly white colleges.[22] Considered the "capstone of Negro education," Howard was never meant to be and would never become a center of learning on a par with the Harvards of the nation. Though Howard had numerous intellectual and scholarly stars on its faculty, the intellectual culture of the institution was somewhat stifling. Ernest Just, the great cell biologist who taught at Howard University, had to fight college administrators from stealing his research funds, which had been awarded to him via outside granting agencies.[23] When reflecting on his days as a member of the History Department of Howard University, John Hope Franklin revealed disappointment in his faculty colleagues and contempt for the scholastically unsupportive university administration:

> The most disturbing thing to me was ... the lack of their determination to become really and truly intellectually independent ... really and truly scholars.... Of course, tied up with that ... is the way the college was operated and the lack of appreciation of scholarship on the part

of those in charge. They never, almost never created a climate that was congenial to it.... It is not without significance that the Howard period is the period in which I did the least of my publishing....[24]

One of the defining moments in the development of these bifurcated black intellectuals occurred when they were forced to realize that the racist restrictions placed on their academic mobility ultimately short-circuited their intellectual ambitions. This realization for Du Bois came during his initial years of teaching at Atlanta University.[25] He had gone to Atlanta University to teach sociology shortly after he had completed the research and writing of the manuscript that would become *The Philadelphia Negro*. Besides teaching, he had come to Atlanta to direct a series of "scientific" studies of Negro life. Excited, he developed elaborate research plans for various empirical studies.

Tragically, Du Bois could never attract foundation funding for his research efforts. Even after *The Philadelphia Negro* was published, Du Bois was not viewed as a researcher worthy of support probably because he was black and intent upon studying blacks. Furthermore, Du Bois's home institution, Atlanta University, was generally not supported by American foundations because it was not adhering to the Hampton Institute/Booker T. Washington pedagogy of industrial training and racial accommodationism.[26] Without sources of external funding, Du Bois knew that he would not be able to realize his considerable research ambitions. Atlanta University did not have the necessary funds to cover the costs of his research agenda. Nevertheless, on less than a shoestring budget, Du Bois conceived, directed, edited, and published numerous Atlanta University sociological studies beginning in 1898.[27] Though the resultant studies were uneven in quality, they were quite respectable. Being able to publish these volumes with so little institutional support may have been one of Du Bois's greatest scholarly achievements.[28]

The Du Bois who arrived at Atlanta University was a committed social scientist. Naively, he believed that the use of rigorous social scientific methods to uncover and document important aspects of black life would challenge and ultimately undermine white racists' beliefs about black life. White racism, he believed, was not supported by social scientific evidence and would ultimately crumble in its wake. It was ignorance that led whites to believe that blacks were their inferiors. Once whites learned the truth about Negroes, the rationale for white supremacy would be weakened. Once the rationale for white supremacy was diminished, whites could begin to engage blacks in a more egalitarian manner.

Du Bois's belief in the emancipatory potential of social science was undermined by the April 1899 lynching of Sam Hose in Georgia. The lynching of this black man led Du Bois to the realization that racism could be effectively confronted only via political engagement. Concerning his response to the lynching, Du Bois wrote:

> Two considerations thereafter broke in upon my work and eventually disrupted it: first, one could not be a calm, cool, and detached scientist while Negroes were lynched, murdered and starved; and secondly, there was no such definite demand for scientific work of the sort that I was doing as I had confidently assumed would be easily forthcoming. I regarded it as axiomatic that the world wanted to learn the truth and if the truth was sought with even approximate accuracy and painstaking devotion, the world would gladly support the effort. This was, of course, but a young man's idealism, not by any means false, but also never universally true.[29]

Though Du Bois had once believed that his use of rigorous social scientific methodology to study the Negro would result in race advancement, he now believed that only racial agitation via political engagement could advance the race. The behavior of white lynchers in collecting body parts of the lynched person was indicative of a racism so thoroughly irrational that it lay beyond the realm of being challenged by facts. Du Bois does not mention the Hose lynching in any detail in *The Souls of Black Folk,* but it clearly served as a motivation behind the text. Perhaps Du Bois does not extensively discuss this lynching in *Souls* because *Souls* was less concerned with black grievances against white racism than with black contributions to American life.

The Souls of Black Folk

Much of the power of *The Souls of Black Folk* stems from its utter deviancy within Afro-American letters. Similarly, much of the aura of Du Bois lies in the fact that he was sui generis and perceived as such by many of his peers. It would be an immense mistake to view *The Souls of Black Folk* as representative of an Afro-American intellectual tradition but no more a mistake than to view the young Du Bois as representative of his contemporary or future Afro-American intellectuals. Instead, *The Souls of Black Folk* could more fruitfully be read as a radical rupture—the self-conscious attempt of one Afro-American thinker not only to conspicuously place the situation of the American Negro within the empathetic, moral, and analytical purview of the Western intellectual tradition but also to bring that Western intellectual tradition within the critical purview of Negro thinkers.[30] Echoing similar sentiments, in 1961, J. Saunders Redding called *Souls* "more history-making than historical" because it "may be seen as fixing that moment in history when the American Negro began to reject the idea of the world's belonging to white people only, and to think of himself, in concert, as a potential force in the organization of society."[31]

Du Bois's desire to bring the entirety of the Western intellectual tradition to bear on the plight of Afro-Americans entailed something very different from the popular reductionisms that constructed the American racial situation into the "Negro problem." Du Bois assumed that the condition of the Negro could only be understood by situating black life within a comprehensive discussion of American society. In so doing, he could use the black lifeworld as a vantage point from which to comment on the entirety of American civilization.[32] While many interpreters of *The Souls of Black Folk* view it as a call to arms for the black "talented tenth," it should also be seen as an invitation to the white "talented tenth" (e.g., "sons of the masters") to bring their erudition and critical faculties to bear on the ways in which they have participated in perpetuating the debased condition of the Negro. Besides the Negro talented tenth, Du Bois's primary audience would have been middle-class northern whites, particularly those who claimed to be liberal on the race question.[33]

Du Bois is thoroughly aggravated by whites who pretend to be sympathetic when metaphorically inquiring of him *how does it feel to be a problem?* Besides its patronizing disingenuousness, the question, how does it feel to be a problem? is defective insofar as it is intent on precluding a comprehensive response. Any truly comprehensive discussion of how does it feel to be a problem? might also ask whites, how does it feel to label blacks as a problem? and/or how does it feel to label blacks as responsible for conditions over which they have little control? In effect, how does it feel to be a problem? rhetorically isolates and then divorces subjugated blacks from their white oppressors. Instead of enticing a comprehensive critique of American society and culture, how does it feel to be a problem? narrows the focal point to the individual or group qualities of blacks.

Du Bois clearly recognizes that the question is really a stigmatization masquerading as an inquiry.

Unlike many of his Afro-American forebears, including Frederick Douglass, Du Bois was not intent on squeezing the history of the Negroes into those master narratives that fathomed the United States as an unfinished but evolving would-be democratic nation. Throughout Douglass's corpus, there are a plethora of statements of how the reality of life for blacks in the United States does not live up to the nation's ideals.[34] There are conspicuously few places in *Souls* where Du Bois invokes the idealism of the Declaration of Independence, the Bill of Rights, or other foundational American documents or master narratives. Nor, for that matter, are there extended discussions of the thoughts of the founding fathers (à la Thomas Jefferson, James Madison). Du Bois's faith in enlightenment values was grounded in the European enlightenment and not its American offspring. As an undergraduate and graduate student, he had momentarily maintained this valorization of European enlightenment values despite the fact that Europeans were using these values and discourses to justify their colonial domination of nonwhite peoples.[35] It was his freedom from blatant racism while in Germany that influenced Du Bois to believe that some European countries (particularly Germany) were truer bearers of enlightenment values than the United States.[36]

Though the young Du Bois recognizes that many educated Americans, particularly educated white Americans of his era, would view him as an outsider to the Western intellectual tradition, he conspicuously does not define himself as a cultural interloper. In Du Bois's mind, the best of the Western intellectual tradition, including the highest of Western high culture, is available to him simply because he appreciates it. There are no racial restrictions to the riches of Western thought. Concerning his own immersion in Western high culture and its acceptance of him, Du Bois writes:

> I sit with Shakespeare and he winces not. Across the color line I move arm in arm with Balzac and Dumas, where smiling men and welcoming women glide in gilded halls. From out the caves of evening that swing between the strong-limbed earth and the tracery of the stars, I summon Aristotle and Aurelius and what soul I will, and they come all graciously with no scorn nor condescension. So, wed with Truth, I dwell above the Veil.[37]

While the American veil (the color line) restricted his physicality, Du Bois intellectually escaped the limitations of the veil by engaging the realm of ideas.

The Souls of Black Folk is not only an immensely difficult book to decipher but a particularly difficult text to contextualize because it is part autobiography, part sociology, part history, part fiction, and part polemic—all of which are filtered through the philosophical worldview of German idealism.[38] Cornel West claims that *Souls* is indebted to pragmatism while Ross Posnock argues that *Souls* embodies an unresolved tension between pragmatism and Hegelianism.[39] In other words, in order to reconstruct the intellectual canvas that confronted Du Bois, one must be conversant in American intellectual and social history. In addition, the student of *Souls* should be familiar with the history of black Americans in addition to the history of dominant racist images of black Americans. And if this is still not enough interpretive homework, the discerning reader of *The Souls of Black Folk* would benefit from a familiarity with the broader developments in antebellum and post-Emancipation Afro-American culture.

In his extraordinary study *To Wake the Nations: Race in the Making of American Literature,* Eric Sundquist has employed his mastery of these various historical contexts in order to write insightfully about the musical notations that appear at the beginning of each chapter of *The Souls of Black Folk.*[40] Lifted from Negro spirituals or what Du Bois called "the sorrow songs," these musical notations are juxtaposed on the printed page with literary quotations from canonical Western texts such as the Bible or the writings of Schiller, Byron, and Elizabeth Barrett Browning, among others. The names of these writers appear beneath their quotations but the titles of the sorrow songs do not appear beneath their musical notations. The lyrics that could have accompanied the musical notations are also absent. Though Du Bois informed his readers in his preface that the musical notations were from sorrow songs, he goes to extraordinary lengths to prevent their recognition as specific songs. The reader of *The Souls of Black Folk* must wait until the last chapter before Du Bois reveals the specific names of the songs affiliated with the musical notations. Had Du Bois not informed the reader of the names of the songs represented by those musical notations, it is unlikely that most readers of *Souls,* then or now, would have been able to associate the musical notations with titles of specific songs.

Why did Du Bois not include lyrics or song titles with the musical notations of the sorrow songs? Some scholars believe that the lyrics were omitted from the text because they would have appeared in black dialect. They assert that Du Bois believed that most educated Americans (black and white) would have found it ludicrous to juxtapose black dialect song lyrics with the cultivated wordings of quotes from classical Western literature.[41] Such juxtaposition might have naively appealed to and erroneously reinforced the racist devaluation of the sorrow songs. Du Bois biographer David Levering Lewis has argued that Du Bois was attempting to raise the status of the Negro spirituals by situating them alongside highbrow European and American verse. Lewis has written:

> Du Bois would carry throughout the volume the device of pairing Negro spirituals with European verse.... He twinned them in this manner in order to advance the then-unprecedented notion of the creative parity and complementarity of white folk and black folk alike. Du Bois meant the cultural symbolism of these double epigraphs to be profoundly subversive of the cultural hierarchy of his time.... Two years into yet another century of seemingly unassailable European supremacy, *Souls* countered with the voices of the dark submerged and unheard.... Until his readers appreciated the message of the songs sung in bondage by black people, Du Bois was saying, the words written in freedom by white people would remain hollow and counterfeit.[42]

Lewis's belief that Du Bois was asserting his cosmopolitanism by insinuating the complementarity of the Negro spirituals and Western classics is quite plausible but does not help to explain why Du Bois did not reveal the names of the songs beneath their musical notations. He could have supplied the titles of the songs without reproducing lyrics in black dialect or otherwise. Perhaps Du Bois withheld the names of the songs as an arrogant act of humbling his reading audience. By including musical notations without identifying the songs from which they were derived, Du Bois probably enticed many readers to assume that they should have been able to identify these tunes. It would have been reasonable for readers to assume that an author would have included musical notations without lyrics and song titles only if those songs and lyrics were sufficiently well-known and easily deduced from the musical notations. As Du Bois undoubtedly intended, most readers were probably stumped and could not decipher the meaning of the notes. Out of ignorance, others simply disregarded the musical notations and went straight to the written text. In both instances, Du Bois was able to assert his cultural superiority over that of his white and black readerships for only he (and very few others) could claim to be at home in as varied a world of cultures.

Still, I wonder how those songs referred to by the musical notations actually sounded. Much of my ignorance of the sound of these songs is but a result of never having heard them in their original forms. How many contemporaries of Du Bois had actually heard these songs sung in their original styles? Even when my annotated edition of *Souls* informs me that the musical notations are from a song with a familiar title such as "My Lord, What a Mourning" or "Swing Low, Sweet Chariot," I know that I have never heard these songs sung in the manner that Du Bois heard them. The real sounds of the sorrow songs have been lost to us via generations of black acculturation. So when I read the foreword to an edition of *Souls* written by the contemporary Afro-American novelist John Edgar Wideman, in which he claimed to have heard versions of the sorrow songs sung in his Philadelphia church while growing up, I realized that Wideman spoke out of ignorance.[43] Whether we "know" these songs from our childhood memories of having heard versions sung by the choir Wings Over Jordan at the local Shiloh Baptist Church or the hyper-refined versions sung by contemporary Fisk Jubilee Singers, we have never heard Du Bois's sorrow songs. They are lost to history. Furthermore, it is not clear that Du Bois had ever heard the songs as they were originally sung. Insofar as he uses Western musical notations in reference to the songs, Du Bois indicates that he was not engaging the original music. Attempts to capture the sorrow songs in formal Western musical notations failed. Sorrow songs with Western musical notations were, in effect, distorted copies of the original.

Reading *The Souls of Black Folk* allows us a glimpse of the early development of Du Bois. I am less certain than others that the issues confronted by Du Bois in this collection of essays prefigure the entirety of his intellectual corpus. Instead, I am a bit more certain that Du Bois's intellectual journey should be read as a series of intellectual fissures, ruptures, and reformulations that reflect a man constantly adapting to altering historical circumstances. Perhaps the only linchpin that connects these revisions and ruptures throughout Du Bois's life is his resilient commitment to the Afro-American freedom struggle, a freedom struggle that will be reconceptualized numerous times in Du Bois's mind.

The author of *The Souls of Black Folk* is a "man for the people" and not a "man of the people." Du Bois would never be a man of the people in the sense that a Booker T. Washington and a Martin Luther King, Jr., were men of the people. I say this even though men of the people are rarely "one of the people." Leaders who imagine themselves as men of the people still differentiate themselves from the masses whom they are shepherding. After all, they have to believe that they are justified in assuming a leadership role.[44]

In *The Souls of Black Folk,* Du Bois composed a text in which he used the most arcane language of his age to defend and advocate for a people who are popularly viewed as uncivilized and perhaps uncivilizable, at least to the degree that "cultured" white Americans imagined themselves as civilized. The arcane language employed by Du Bois in *The Souls of Black Folk* was archaic even for his day.[45] Paradoxically, Du Bois's arcane language simultaneously advances and compromises his political project. Du Bois uses arcane language in a bid to claim a status that he deems rightfully his, the "man-of-culture." According to literary critic Houston Baker, Matthew Arnold was among the creators of the ideal of the man-of-culture. In providing a thick description of the idea of the man-of-culture, Baker writes:

> For DuBois and Arnold, culture consisted of the study of harmonious perfection and the acquisition and diffusion of "the best that has been thought and known in the world ... [in order] to make all men live in an atmosphere of sweetness and light."[46] It encompassed a knowledge of the classics, a grounding in the broad human sympathies, and a struggle for self-realization through the arts of the Western world. The cultured man is elevated above the scenes of clerical and secular life; he is at some remove from the people, a man of astute sensibility who can wisely and justly criticize the state of society.[47]

At the time of the publication of *The Souls of Black Folk,* Du Bois was probably one of the most formally educated individuals in the United States. His refined style of writing (some might call it affected) is reminiscent of efforts by earlier generations of blacks to use literacy as proof of Afro-American humanity. Whereas Du Bois is not using literacy to prove black humanity, he appears intent on proving that blacks could be cultivated. But Du Bois's language creates a profound tension that saturates *Souls.* Though he wants to be recognized as an authentic man-of-culture, a designation that at that time meant (and perhaps still does) a person fluent in highbrow

European culture, he simultaneously desires that his style and cultural literacy be acknowledged without severing him from the group in behalf of whom he writes.

But how does Du Bois resolve the tension between his personal refinement and highbrow cultivation and the absence of cultural cultivation among the majority of black people? Du Bois clearly recognizes that his representativeness of Negroes may be questioned by his readership precisely because he is so culturally different from most blacks. As if to immediately address this concern, in the preface to *Souls* (The Forethought), Du Bois asserts his racial organicity: "And need I add that I who speak here am bone of the bone and flesh of the flesh of them that live within the Veil."[48]

"*And need I add*" is a clever rhetorical ploy that insinuates that it is perhaps unnecessary for Du Bois to make a claim about his ties to blacks, a claim that he knows is utterly necessary. But merely stating that he is "bone of the bone" with the rest of black Americans does not prove that he is. If anything, Du Bois's need to proclaim his racial bona fides implies that he thought they might be questioned.

Certainly, there was no similar statement emanating from Booker T. Washington in *Up From Slavery*, which had been published a few years before *The Souls of Black Folk*. Washington's racial ties to the masses of blacks were taken for granted. Having been born a slave, Washington's black organicity was beyond question. Besides, Washington's public persona had been constructed so as to reinforce images of black humility, service, and deference to whites. He purposely avoided styles of dress, oratory, and literary elegance that could have been interpreted as "uppity." In his personal style, he communicated those idealized images that white Americans projected onto all Negroes and thus reinforced the sense that he was organically "one of them."

On the other hand, Du Bois had to forestall in his readership the idea that he was a racial deviant if his thoughts were to be accepted as representative of widespread Negro concerns and sensibilities. He simultaneously wanted and did not want to be considered unique.[49] He was proud of his cultural uniqueness though fearful of its potential political consequences. Du Bois was culturally deviant vis-à-vis other blacks, but he was politically "in the same boat" with them. After all, his cultural status and refinement did not elevate his political status. Ironically, Du Bois believed that his cultured status should have differentiated him from the black masses in the eyes of whites. He had argued in *The Philadelphia Negro* that one of the problems hindering black progress was the fact that whites did not recognize the "black elite" and grant them the power to lead and uplift the race.[50]

Du Bois as Exceptional Man

Despite Du Bois's ambivalence about minimizing his linkages to the uncultivated and uncultured black masses, *The Souls of Black Folk* can perhaps be understood as an attempt on the part of one black man to proclaim individuality in the face of a suffocating culture of racist homogenization. Most contemporary interpreters of *Souls* believe that the book encompasses so much more than a self-centered bid for individualization. Though justifiably perceiving civic-mindedness in *The Souls of Black Folk,* these critics often lose sight of the aspirations of individualization that are central to the book. Astute readers of *Souls* immediately perceive that Du Bois not only recognizes himself as exceptional but also conveys his singularity through his use of language. Personally proud of his exceptionality, Du Bois is politically ambivalent about its ramifications. Perhaps it is no surprise then that in *The Souls of Black Folk* this exceptionality assumes three distinct configurations that at times conflict with each other. Three ideas of exceptionality that appear in *Souls* (sometimes repeatedly) are:

1. the generic idea of Du Bois as exceptional because he is a high achiever;
2. the idea of Du Bois as exceptional because he is a high achiever on account of being a Negro; and
3. the idea of Du Bois as exceptional because he is a high achiever despite being a Negro.

The least conspicuous but most ubiquitous form of exceptionality affiliated with *Souls* is premised on Du Bois's impressive personal achievements. Possessing a Harvard B.A. and Ph.D., undertaking further graduate study in Germany, and publishing two well-received books, *The Suppression of the African Slave Trade to the United States of America, 1638–1870* in 1896 and *The Philadelphia Negro: A Social Study* in 1899, were certainly grounds to recognize Du Bois as exceptional, but only superficially. This form of exceptionality is not associated with racial identity. Any white American who had attained similar degrees and published similar manuscripts at such a young age would have been deemed exceptional. And this is precisely the problem! In confronting Du Bois's implicit claim to the status of exceptional, a hidden implication emerges that Du Bois may have achieved on the same level as a high-achieving white person. Du Bois the black writer becomes potentially analogous to a white man of letters. An omnipresent, though never mentioned, white shadow hovers over the entirety of *Souls* precisely because the book is so Du Boisian (read *whitelike*). Du Bois's chutzpah, as evident in his life's achievements, inconspicuously invokes a favorable comparison to whites and whiteness. In having the audacity to write about his exceptional life, Du Bois conspicuously violates his racial caste. *Just who does this Negro think he is?* Posnock writes: "In turning his being a 'thing apart' from a condition of abjection into one of compelling originality, Du Bois appropriated a weapon of racist control and classification—the weapon of 'distinction'—for his own use."[51]

It is this first configuration of exceptionality that grants Du Bois the cultural authority to make demands on the literary interests of white and black readers. Without his association with this first type of exceptionality, most people in turn-of-the-century America would never have entertained the idea of reading *The Souls of Black Folk*. Unlike *Up From Slavery,* which was written by the universally acknowledged leader of the Negro race, *Souls* was written by a Negro who, though well-known as a writer, had no claim to race leadership. At the time of the publication of *The Souls of Black Folk,* it was a rare event for a black author to have his books published by a major white publishing house. It was trickier still for a Negro American author to publish a book about the "race problem" in America and attempt to engage simultaneously white and black reading audiences. That many of the essays that comprise *Souls* had been previously published in major mass-circulation "white" magazines only helped to enhance the credibility of Du Bois's book. Previous publication in white-edited magazines certified that other whites, presumably those in the know, had thought Du Bois worth reading.

The second type of exceptionality found in *Souls* organically links Du Bois to his race. In this guise, Du Bois is exceptional because he has realized outstanding achievements and has done so because he is a Negro. In this guise of exceptionality, Du Bois becomes the Emersonian representative man of his racial group for he embodies the group's potentialities.[52] Something within the Negro world successfully pushed and prodded him to achieve. It was as if Du Bois had gotten in touch with the racial genius that he and all other Negroes carried within themselves. Given similar opportunities, other Negroes could achieve what Du Bois has achieved. Du Bois markets this image of exceptionality when he writes that his intellectual outlook is as much a response to his life behind the veil as it is his life among Western thinkers. In *Dusk of Dawn,* published years after *The Souls of Black Folk,* Du Bois stated that there were potentially many more exceptional black men. He noted that "down among the mass, ten times their number with equal ability could be discovered and developed" if the effort was exerted.[53]

The third configuration of exceptionality found in *The Souls of Black Folk* presupposes that Du Bois is exceptional in spite of being a Negro. In this instance, exceptionality is deemed rare among Negroes. Du Bois, that rare Negro, is "unlike the others." Du Bois knows that he is culturally unlike most blacks but he does not desire to use his uniqueness as a mechanism to divorce himself from the group. He knows that he cannot possibly rally the Negro talented tenth to take up the mantle of race leadership if he is viewed as claiming that he is different from and/or superior to the "other blacks." Du Bois realizes that in the United States, there is no social or cultural benefit for claiming the status of "the Negro who is unlike the others." Though some whites may have viewed a Negro like Du Bois as being unlike the other blacks, they did not allow this racial exceptionality to translate into increased rights for the deviant Negro. Unlike those Jews in post-emancipated Europe who used their status as being "unlike the other Jews" to gain a parvenu social mobility, would-be black parvenus in the late nineteenth-century United States were not allowed to racially differentiate themselves from other blacks.[54]

Du Bois could have never openly admitted that he entertained ideas about being "unlike the other blacks." To publicly acknowledge such would have undermined any hope he had of leading the race or even speaking for it. As such, Du Bois does not will to use his exceptional status in order to be seen as a tragic individual. He is not the metaphorical precursor of the tragic mulatto, too culturally white to be at home comfortably with blacks and too stained by race to be accepted by whites [read *"cultured" whites*].[55] Nevertheless, his cultural distaste for the black masses is repeatedly displayed in *Souls.*[56]

Du Bois's strategy for resolving this tension lies in his adoption of German idealism. Borrowing from the ideas of Hegel and Herder,

Du Bois wills himself to be the exceptional Negro who embodies the forward-leaning ethos of his people. Though exceptional, he is representative of the potentialities of his people. The exceptional man/woman, in embodying the cultural/spiritual ethos of the folk, will elevate the folk to their justifiable place on the world stage of accomplished cultures. The folk are essential for they create the cultural uniqueness and spirit through which the man-of-culture is inspired. In this sense, the man-of-culture and the folk are mutually parasitic. The folk create the spiritedness that will give the man-of-culture his cultural "raw materials." The man-of-culture gives the folk their most refined voice. Only he can make fine art out of folk art. The man-of-culture and the folk need each other if they are ever to realize their unique historical calling: the elevation of their race.[57]

But Du Bois faces a further problem. In the prevailing hierarchy of peoples and cultures, black Americans (and for that matter, Africans) were not granted the status of being a "folk." Certainly, they were not thought of as folk in the same romanticized manner that European peasants were viewed as folk. Black peoples are viewed as having created nothing of significant cultural value. They have not produced the cultural raw materials upon which a man-of-culture could chisel something of enduring beauty and value. So Du Bois has a herculean task before him. He has to validate himself as a man-of-culture while simultaneously validating black Americans as a folk and thus the source of vital creativity and his own cultural uniqueness. Du Bois's ability to claim a Herderian exceptional-man status depends upon the successful construction of the black American neopeasantry as a "folk."[58]

Notwithstanding, Du Bois is not a strict German idealist. He is also very American in his political-philosophical sensibilities. As a consequence, he simultaneously embraces German idealism and American pragmatism.[59] Though thoroughly romantic, Du Bois is not interested in the folk merely because they provide him with raw cultural materials. He also recognizes their humanity, a humanity that is apparent in their souls, their humane essences, which is perceivable through their Sorrow Songs. The suffering of black Americans is tragic and Du Bois despises whites for their treatment of blacks. The situation of black Americans was tragic precisely because blacks possessed heroic qualities: their humanness and cultural creativity. Du Bois's depiction of Negro Americans as tragic was but one rhetorical brick hurled against the social Darwinism of his day, a social Darwinism that viewed the subjugated status of blacks as inevitable due to their natural inferiority.[60] Another brick hurled at social Darwinism was Du Bois's personal example—an example that implicitly calls forth the possibility that there could be many other black people-of-culture if they would but have the opportunity to pursue formal education.

In Du Bois's mind, black folk will never progress if they are not given opportunity. Opportunity cannot be secured until the folk are released from their imprisonment to the land as neoserfs. This advancement could occur only if Negroes were granted the protection and benefits of full citizenship. But full citizenship, though necessary, was not sufficient. Blacks must also be educated to the fullest extent of their talents. Du Bois believes that those blacks who are capable of becoming men- and women-of-culture should be encouraged to do so. Industrial education will be sufficient for many blacks, but it would be a travesty to deny others a liberal arts education. Du Bois postulates an unstated but ever-present intraracial division of labor in pursuit of the race's cultural advancement.[61] But Du Bois wants a serious liberal arts education for as many blacks as possible. He recognizes the low level of education offered in most black colleges of his day and considers them the equivalent of high schools.

Du Bois would never uncritically celebrate the growth in the number of blacks attaining college degrees though, for tactical reasons, he recognized that any degree of education was better than none. In *The Souls of Black Folk,* he wrote: "The advocates of higher education of the Negro would be the last to deny the incompleteness and glaring defects of the present system: too many institutions have attempted to do college work, the work in some cases has not been thoroughly done, and quantity rather than quality has sometimes been sought."[62]

Blacks with college degrees were worthy of celebration if and only if they had been substantively educated. At the time of the publication of *Souls,* most black colleges were not producing substantively educated graduates. Yet, a few predominantly black institutions were training quality graduates (e.g., Atlanta University, Howard, Fisk, Lincoln, Wilberforce, Biddle,[63] and Shaw).[64] Du Bois noted that about two thousand Negroes had been trained by these institutions.[65] Also included by Du Bois in the ranks of the substantively educated were those four hundred living Negroes who had graduated from Harvard, Yale, Oberlin, and other elite, predominantly white colleges.[66] Only substantively educated blacks could fulfill the mission of what we might today call a "race intelligentsia."

In Du Bois's mind, this professionalized race intelligentsia would simultaneously function as a community of nascent "transformative intellectuals."[67] As transformative intellectuals, it was the duty of the professionalized black intelligentsia to step outside their professional roles and advocate for the rights of blacks and respond to racist assaults on black American humanity. Du Bois contended that ethnic uplift was a core component of privileged black existence, though he also recognized that many among the "better element" of Negroes would not embrace such responsibilities. Du Bois assumed that the responsible members of the Negro talented tenth would outnumber those privileged blacks who believed that vacation homes on Oak Bluffs and memberships in various fraternities or sororities constituted noteworthy achievements.

Du Bois understood that black men- and women-of-culture would feel estranged from the broader black masses. He lived that estrangement. He also recognized that in their estrangement, black men- and women-of-culture might entertain doubts about the creative potential of the race. One must understand the idea of two-ness within this context. It was the unique angst of the black man- and woman-of-culture.[68]

Exceptionalism and Estrangement

In the essay "Of Our Spiritual Strivings," Du Bois penned his now famous metaphor of black life.

> After the Egyptian and Indian, the Greek and Roman, the Teuton and Mongolian, the Negro is a sort of seventh son, born with a veil, and gifted with second sight in his American world, a world that yields him no true self-consciousness, but only lets him see himself through the revelation of the other world. It is a peculiar sensation, this double consciousness, this sense of always looking at one's self through the eyes of others, of measuring one's soul by the type of a world that looks on in amused contempt and pity. One ever feels his two-ness, an American, a Negro; two souls, two thoughts, two unreconciled strivings; two warring ideals in one dark body, whose dogged strength alone keeps it from being torn asunder.
>
> The history of the American Negro is the history of this strife, this longing to attain self-conscious manhood, to merge his double self into a better and truer self. In this merging he wishes neither of the older selves to be lost. He would not Africanize America, for America

has too much to teach the world and Africa. He would not bleach his Negro soul in a flood of white Americanism, for he knows that Negro blood has a message for the world. He simply wishes to make it possible for a man to be both a Negro and an American, without being cursed and spit upon by his fellows, without having the doors of opportunity closed roughly in his face.[69]

Du Bois's belief that blacks had not arrived at true self-consciousness because of their inability to cease viewing themselves through the lens of white American perceptions appears heavily indebted to Hegel.[70] In *The Phenomenology of Mind,* Hegel discussed the importance of mutual recognition in his master-slave paradigm.[71] Du Bois had studied Hegel's thought at Harvard in a class taught by philosopher George Santayana.[72] Later, he would have confronted Hegelianism again as a graduate student at the University of Berlin during the early 1890s.[73]

But what did Du Bois mean by double consciousness?[74]

Many students of Du Bois have assumed that he was generally describing the fact that blacks, though American, were outsiders in American society. Though blacks were American citizens and deeply embedded in American political idealism, they were denied the opportunity to realize these ideals socially, economically, legally, and politically. Essentially, they were denied full citizenship rights. Other scholars have interpreted Du Bois as describing a dual cultural identity. Blacks were deemed culturally American and yet non-American, Western and yet non-Western. Du Bois appears to give credence to this interpretation with his claim that the American Negro would neither "Africanize America" nor "bleach his Negro soul" in a flood of white Americanism. Desire aside, was the American Negro in 1903 sufficiently "African" to have been able to Africanize America? Du Bois appears intent on describing blacks as participants in a tension of dual cultural allegiance, but to do so he is forced to exaggerate the degree to which all Negroes were culturally non-American. In what ways could Du Bois have been described as culturally African?

It seems equally likely that Du Bois meant none of the above. Instead, one could read Du Bois's double-consciousness metaphor as premised upon a belief in racial essentialisms in which races were deemed to be innate carriers of particular values, traditions, and artistic gifts. Racial essentialism abounds in *The Souls of Black Folk* and was prefigured in Du Bois's earlier essay "The Conservation of Races."[75] Such an argument would make more sense of Du Bois's desire not to Africanize America and could explain how Du Bois, a Europhile, maintained a resilient belief in his Africanness.[76]

Given the variety of interpretations of the double-consciousness metaphor, one point of consistency in these various interpretations stems from the probability that Du Bois could only have been writing about Negroes like himself. Shamoon Zamir makes this point more emphatically:

> The frequency with which Du Bois's description is used suggests that it is commonly accepted as a universally and transhistorically true analysis of a tragic aspect of African-American self-consciousness. But Du Bois's dramatization of "double-consciousness" is a historically specific and class specific psychology. The account of "double-consciousness" in the first chapter of *Souls* represents the black middle-class elite facing the failure of its own progressive ideals in the late nineteenth century, in the aftermath of failed Reconstruction and under the gaze of a white America. "Of Our Spiritual Strivings" is intended as a psychology of the Talented Tenth in crisis, not of the "black folk" as a homogenized collectivity.[77]

Only a Negro who was sufficiently embedded in and consciously conversant with highbrow Western culture and/or American political ideals could have experienced Du Bois's double consciousness. As a result, *The Souls of Black Folk* can be read as a testament of the peculiar social dislocation experienced by a late nineteenth-, early twentieth-century black man-of-culture, who, for reasons of race, is denied his rightfully earned opportunity to participate in advancing American civilization.

The Souls of Black Folk can be fruitfully interpreted as the plea of an individual who, as a member of an oppressed group, dislikes the way that the oppressor treats his people but simultaneously believes that the majority of his people are not culturally ready to assume the full responsibilities of freedom. Du Bois, in being "cultured," is deserving of equal recognition from whites but is denied equality by an oppressor too racist to make distinctions among Negroes and too indifferent to black humanity to allow cultured Negroes, like himself, the opportunity to "uplift the civilization" of his race.[78]

Essentially, Du Bois experiences the ambivalences of a man who lives the life of a victim but who valorizes the idealized culture of the victimizer. The double-consciousness metaphor can therefore be understood as a simplified reformulation of Hegel's master-slave paradigm.[79] The slave, in this instance Du Bois (or "cultured" Negroes as a group), continually craves recognition of his humanity from the master (read *"cultured" white America*). The quest for white recognition is crucial. Only certain whites, always imagined as "cultured" whites, and the few "cultured" blacks can appreciate the fine sensibilities of the black man-of-culture. Though other cultured blacks recognized his status, Du Bois solicited recognition from the only recognizers that mattered, cultured whites. His deference to cultured whites is not solely the result of his highbrow Eurocentric consciousness but also a pragmatic assessment of the power that whites held over blacks. Apparently, Du Bois felt that those white American elites most deeply steeped in Western humanistic values constituted that sector of white elites most apt to be morally concerned about the condition of blacks.

As a black man-of-culture, Du Bois detests his treatment by whites and is deeply angered by the unwillingness of elite cultured whites to grant him and other cultured Negroes the recognition, authority, and resources necessary to cultivate their people. Du Bois views the racist treatment of blacks in the South as nothing less than barbaric. Fortunately, there exist moral-minded whites in the North and South, "the sons of the masters," who can be appealed to in hopes of altering that situation.[80] Herein lies the tortured ambiguity of Du Bois's double consciousness. Du Bois wants blacks as a collective entity to realize their moment in history, but he does not deem white Americans worthy of black emulation precisely because of the way they have treated blacks. Given his racially premised, culturally essentialist views, Du Bois believed that blacks had a unique gift to offer to world cultural advancement. Consequently, Du Bois is not an assimilationist. He is acculturated to the extent that Western humanist ideals, the ideals professed but not practiced by elite white Americans, are the very ideals that he celebrates and desires to teach black Americans. One cannot understand the richness of *The Souls of Black Folk* without confronting the anguished, almost racially/culturally obsequious, status-grasping motivations in Du Bois's use of arcane, highbrow Western humanistic language.

The voice that Du Bois appropriates in the hope of generating a serious reading of his text is supposedly used in the service of racial uplift. One could just as easily reverse the reading and argue that the elitist Du Bois was using the plight of the subjugated black neopeasantry as a backdrop to highlight the uniqueness of his own problematic status as a black man-of-culture. While a defense of the race, *The Souls of Black Folk* also embodies Du Bois's bid for the status of the exceptional Negro ("he who is unlike the others").

Now it may appear problematic to argue that Du Bois simultaneously viewed the Afro-American situation through the eyes of the victim and the victimizer, for Du Bois unequivocally intended politically to side with the oppressed. Yet, in endorsing and reproducing criteria for black enfranchisement that had historically kept blacks off the voting rolls, Du Bois appropriates the values of the victimizer to assess the victim. Concerning the attitude of cultured Negroes toward the "uncultured" black southern peasant, Du Bois wrote, "They do not ask that ignorant black men vote when ignorant whites are debarred, or that any reasonable restrictions in the suffrage should not be applied; they know that the low social level of the mass of the race is responsible for much discrimination against it, but they also know and the nation knows, that relentless color prejudice is more often a cause than a result of the Negro's degradation...."[81]

Du Bois believes that, unlike himself, most blacks of his day were unfit for suffrage. However, he also believes that "ignorant" whites should be denied suffrage. If whites were denied political participation based on the same criteria used to disenfranchise blacks, Du Bois was all but ready to label such criteria rational. In this respect, Du Bois assumes the voice of the victimizer attempting to rationalize inequality along class lines. More importantly, if he believes that black cultural degradation is primarily caused by white racism and that blacks who are culturally degraded should not have the right to vote, Du Bois ultimately legitimates the implications of racism. His double consciousness forces him to simultaneously blame the subjugated and the oppressor for the plight of the oppressed. Du Bois appears to momentarily confuse the social rationalization of racial inequality with the causes of racial inequality.

A hidden major presumption in *Souls* is that Du Bois was unjustly denied certain rights that other blacks were justifiably denied. Again, this line of argument comes far too close to a bid for the status of "exceptional Negro." The exceptional Negro is caught between his blackness and his whiteness, or put another way, between his race and his Western acculturation (read *whiteness*).[82] But Du Bois is also trapped between his desire for white recognition and his anger at whites. In his admission that many blacks are not qualitatively ready for full citizenship rights, he intends to reassure reasonable whites that they are in fact reasonable and that he is, too. It is a bid for individual acceptance. Du Bois intends to distinguish himself from those unreasonable Negroes such as Monroe Trotter and Ida B. Wells who are ridiculously demanding equality and immediate voting rights for all blacks. In the quest for personal recognition, moderation is often the calling card of the subjugated caught in the ambivalent quest for their oppressor's recognition.

Jessie Fauset, the black female novelist who would later gain prominence during the Harlem Renaissance, celebrated Du Bois for his exceptionalism. After reading *The Souls of Black Folk* in 1903, she wrote Du Bois a congratulatory note that, in essence, claimed that the black man-of-culture and woman-of-culture suffered more at the hands of racism than the everyday black: "I am glad you wrote it—we have needed someone to voice the intricacies of the blind maze of thought and action along which the modern, educated colored man or woman struggles. It hurt you to write that book didn't it? The man of fine sensibilities has to suffer exquisitely, just simply because his feeling is so fine."[83]

The issue of concern here is not the authenticity of Du Bois's suffering at the hands of American racism. Certainly, he suffered, but it is not clear that Du Bois suffered more than illiterate southern black sharecroppers. Fauset's claim, however, rests on the hidden presupposition that the "cultured" (read *Westernized*) black person was especially sensitive to and unfit for such degrading treatment. The unstated major premise of her argument is that uncultured blacks had not developed the emotional capabilities to experience suffering in all of its grandeur. They were better fit for suffering!

Du Bois's self-consciously elitist bid to occupy the status of the exceptional Negro explicitly attempted to assault the popularly held belief that blacks were incapable of attaining what was then thought to be high cultural refinement. His use of highbrow cultural refinement as a weapon against racist degradations of black peoples is but a higher-order version of those attempts by earlier generations of black Americans to use literacy as proof of their human equality. Imagine the discontinuity in the minds of some whites who recognized that Du Bois, in appropriating an air of highbrow Eurocentric sophistication, called into question the pretensions of a culturally impoverished America dominated by Philistine white "captains of industry." Paradoxically, Du Bois's assault on a white racist image of blacks took place within an appeal that essentially claimed that most black Americans were not culturally ready to assume the responsibilities and benefits of full citizenship.

Traces of Du Bois's elitism and self-centered quest for the designation of exceptional Negro can be found throughout *The Souls of Black Folk*. Too many contemporary students of Du Bois attempt to read *Souls* as if it is proto–*Wretched of the Earth* and in so doing discard the complexities of the text. *Souls* is riddled with ambivalence. It not only is concerned with the liberation of the Negro people, it also projects the desire on the part of one black intellectual to differentiate himself from the crude masses of his people. Du Bois may have willed himself to join the Afro-American freedom struggle but not at the expense of pretending that all Negroes were his equal. In *Souls,* Du Bois had written: "I should be the last one to deny the patent weaknesses and shortcomings of the Negro people.... I freely acknowledge that it is possible, and sometimes best, that a partially undeveloped people should be ruled by the best of their stronger and better neighbors for their own good, until such time as they can start and fight the world's burdens alone."[84]

Du Bois's elitism may well have been a functional component of his intellectual style and ambitions. Given his extraordinary deviancy as a hypereducated, high-culture Negro American at the dawn of the twentieth century, Du Bois's elitism could have functioned as a protective device of sorts. Unlike some intellectual elitists who were personally quite gregarious with nonelite peoples, Du Bois's elitism also informed his personal interactions with friends and strangers. His demeanor was that of a cold, aloof person. This personal style may have helped to shield him from certain personal boundary violations from whites. He certainly would have wanted to regulate, as much as possible, whites from presuming those familiarities that they often took as a racial prerogative when interacting with Negroes. Moreover, Du Bois's elitism may have helped him to navigate interactions with whites as an equal. Whether whites accepted him as an authentic man-of-culture, Du Bois's personal decorum exuded an aura that informed whites that he viewed himself as their cultural equal, if not superior. His elitist self-definition and demeanor accomplished this without his having to verbally state as much. One can imagine many whites, after meeting Du Bois, proclaiming to themselves and other whites, "Just who does that Negro think he is?"

Du Boisian Reflections on Contemporary Black Intellectuals

Such self-conscious elitism as displayed by Du Bois has long since fallen out of favor within the Afro-American intelligentsia. Today, any black intellectual who aspires to popular legitimacy among blacks could never openly appropriate an "air of superiority." While the demise of conspicuous elitism is a welcome advance within the black intelligentsia, it should not be assumed that egalitarianism has become the governing ethic of contemporary Afro-American intellectuals. Like all traditional intellectuals, Afro-American intellectuals seek to maintain their voices as privileged. The widely celebrated rise of black public intellectuals during the past decade has not been accompanied by a corresponding expansion or intensification of democratic dialogue within Afro-America. Unfortunately, the new black public intellectuals have committed little effort and few resources in creating new public spaces for intellectual exchange within the ethnic group. What is often publicly marketed as oppositional Afro-American intellectual activity is merely a new version of intellectuals speaking in behalf of a community that does not have the power to certify whether or not they are being accurately represented. The ability of Afro-American intellectuals to appropriate the mantle of spokespersons for black America at large is sometimes enhanced by the willingness of these intellectual spokespeople to cleverly appropriate black popular-culture styles of speaking. Style aside, the inequality between the thinker and the public remains.

Insofar as they are attempting to speak for the entire ethnic group without certification from that ethnic group, contemporary black intellectuals are merely reproducing Du Bois's elitism. What is different is that contemporary black intellectuals have a much broader range of venues within which to speak or write. Consequently, their supposed representativeness is now certified and/or rationalized by mainstream American institutions (i.e., national media outlets) in ways that Du Bois could never have imagined. As such, it is ever more difficult to delegitimize these figures as "black spokespeople." Many contemporary Afro-American intellectuals who claim to be antielitist devote less energy to addressing the black poor and working classes than the self-consciously elitist Du Bois. Certainly, there are public intellectuals who do not feel the disdain for the black lower classes that Du Bois felt. Nonetheless, it does not appear that this affinity for and with the black poor has generated novel forms of public intellectual engagement.[85]

Undoubtedly, the young scholar who penned *The Souls of Black Folk* could not have imagined the contemporary situation of Afro-American intellectuals in the United States. One hundred years after the publication of *Souls,* there has been a virtual sea change in the number of blacks who have obtained higher education and/or have engaged the life of the mind. With the reduction in the viciousness of the white racist exclusion of blacks from centers of higher educa tion and professional "intellectual" positions (e.g., writers for major newspapers and magazines, editors at publishing houses, staff of foundations), the size of the black intelligentsia has expanded. This progress should not be cause for celebration for, when *The Souls of Black Folk* was published, there were probably fewer than ten Afro-American Ph.D.s in the entire United States.[86] Increases in the numbers of blacks obtaining Ph.D.s during the course of the twentieth century do not in and of themselves tell us a great deal about the qualitative inclusion of black intellectuals today.

One of the major changes in Afro-American intellectual life (and perhaps American intellectual life in general) that has occurred during the twentieth century has been a significant lessening of the deference given to European cultures.[87] The rise of the American century following World War II, when coupled with an increased awareness of European barbarism (i.e., the Holocaust), undermined the uncritical valorization of European cultures within American intellectual life. During this same period, American scholars were becoming more respectful of American cultural creativity. The twentieth-century Afro-American intellectual devalorization of European cultures was further stimulated by the rise of third-world anticolonial movements, particularly African liberation movements. During the first six decades of the twentieth century, no single American intellectual figure did more than Du Bois via scholarship and polemic to support African decolonization. Even in the aftermath of World War II, the European colonial dominance of colored peoples did not stimulate a critique of Europe within most white American intellectual circles. Within white American intellectual venues, the European dominance of colored peoples continued as the unquestioned natural order of things.[88] Conversely, within Afro-American intellectual circles, the anticolonial struggles of third-world peoples amplified the status of third-world cultures as sources of creative nourishment and inspiration for domestic political engagement.

Throughout the twentieth century, Afro-American intellectuals engaged in various efforts to influence the U.S. government to support African decolonization. The founding of the International Committee on African Affairs (ICAA) in 1937 was a major step in generating an anticolonial pressure front. Founded as an interracial pressure group, ICAA included leftists, liberals, social gospel Christians, and even corporate philanthropists.[89] By 1942, the ICAA would redefine itself as the Council on African Affairs (CAA), an explicitly leftist pressure front. Among its leading figures were Afro-American intellectuals such as Paul Robeson, Max Yergin, Alphaeus Hunton, Jr., and later W. E. B. Du Bois. CAA would remain a vital pressure group until it was destroyed by McCarthy-era anticommunist repression. Following the demise of CAA, the American Committee on Africa (ACOA), a less radical organization, was founded with the intent of generating American popular support for African decolonization.[90] Chaired by a white anticolonialism activist, George Houser, ACOA attracted black intellectuals such as Rayford Logan, James Farmer, and Bayard Rustin.

The mid-1950s also saw the establishment of an African American organization whose mission was to improve the status of Africa in the eyes of the United States by promoting African culture in a positive manner. The American Society of African Culture (AMSAC) was established in the aftermath of the 1956 international conference of black writers held in Paris and sponsored by the journal *Présence Africaine* and the Society for African Culture. Included in AMSAC's membership were Afro-American intellectuals like John Aubrey Davis, Mercer Cook, Horace Mann Bond, William Fontaine, and James Ivy. Whereas CAA had been repressed because of its militant anticolonialism and left-wing affiliations, AMSAC would attract clandestine CIA funding.[91]

From our vantage point at the beginning of the twenty-first century, Africa and African cultures are no longer simply marginalized as exotic and primitive. Today, many, if not most, American institutions of higher learning offer courses in African studies, a fact that testifies to the improved status of Africa in the United States. African studies in the United States owes a tremendous debt to Northwestern University anthropologist Melville Herskovits. Under his leadership, the African Studies Association was founded in 1957.[92] Still, the resources committed to African studies by American academia during the past fifty years do not begin to compare with the resources committed to European studies or Asian studies. Unfortunately, the strengthening of African studies within American academia has been accompanied by only a modest improvement in mass American public concern for the peoples of Africa. Present-day curiosity and compassion for Africa in the American mass public are significantly less than American mass public concern for most other regions of the world. One need only revisit the American political indifference to the genocide in Rwanda or the more recent killing fields in southern and western Sudan. Compare the American moral detachment to the killing in Rwanda with the American intervention in the crisis in the former Yugoslavia.

Whereas African studies formally emerged in the United States during the mid-1950s, Afro-American studies would not emerge until the middle to late 1960s. The creation of Afro-American studies programs (sometimes called black studies or Africana studies) during the late 1960s constituted the first sustained efforts on the part of mainstream American academia to become inclusive of the study of black Americans.[93] It was during this same period that black students were first admitted to predominantly white colleges in significant numbers. These newly admitted black students were in many instances the instigating force behind the creation of Afro-American studies programs.

The establishment of black studies departments led to an increase in the number of Afro-American faculty teaching at predominantly white colleges and universities.[94] Many of these new black faculty on predominantly white campuses were hired from predominantly black colleges. This black brain drain became a significant issue within Afro-American intellectual circles insofar as black professors housed in newly created black studies programs on predominantly white campuses tended to teach fewer black students than they had taught at historically black colleges. Nevertheless, the access to greater resources, lesser teaching loads, higher salaries, and increased research opportunities at predominantly white colleges were enticing to black scholars even though, once arriving on the predominantly white campus, they were often herded into what many there considered to be a segregated, inferior appendage to the traditional academic disciplines.[95]

The racial segregation of a college's faculty became noticeable when black faculty began appearing in black-only or predominantly black Afro-American studies programs and departments. Prior to the 1970s, most academic departments on predominantly white campuses were concertedly racist in their hiring practices.

Furthermore, these departments were not subjected to stigmatization because of their racist practices. Racial segregationist hiring policies in American higher education were so thoroughly standard operating procedure that they went unnoticed, except by the excluded blacks. Once established, black studies programs would become multiply stigmatized because of their association with blackness. They were stigmatized because they were 1) concerned with the study of devalued black peoples; 2) linked to a black student body deemed to be inferior; and 3) home to "less qualified" black faculty. When first established, some black studies programs hired unqualified black faculty.

During the late 1960s, college administrations, in their rush to appear racially inclusive, were often more concerned about obtaining an immediate black faculty physical presence than ascertaining the competency of those present. While there can be no justification for an indifference to intellectual standards when establishing black studies programs, college administrations were often under pressure of black student activists who were primarily interested in bringing black faculty bodies to campus.

Amidst the turmoil surrounding the creation of black studies programs on college campuses, an idea gained currency that any and all black faculty who taught in black studies programs or departments were intellectually inferior. Variations of this argument included "no competent faculty persons, including blacks, would want to be housed in a black studies department"; or "those newly arrived black faculty persons would not have been hired had there not been a nonrigorous black studies program and thus they were unqualified"; or finally, "no competent faculty person would dare to be associated with such a counterfeit scholarly enterprise as black studies." Historical hiring practices grounded in the racist exclusion of black faculty, when not conveniently forgotten, were now being invoked as having had a meritocratic rationale. According to this logic, if black faculty had been qualified, they would have been teaching there all along.

We are left with an absurdity. The only surefire way to prove that the same competency criteria were being applied equally to black and white faculty was not to hire black faculty. If there were no blacks on the faculty, there would be no blacks to distinguish as having been the reason behind a white person's job loss. During the period when black studies programs were founded, an unstated and virtually unchallengeable hidden presupposition of American academia was that existing white faculty were universally qualified. In some respects, the perception of black studies as a serious scholarly arena would not take off until the late 1970s and early 1980s when younger white graduate students and scholars began to venture into this arena. Following a very American pattern, it would take white intellectuals to legitimate black intellectuals in the eyes of other white intellectuals! In this regard, little had changed from the time of the young Du Bois and *The Souls of Black Folk*.

Unfortunately, the association of black studies with black student protest and broader racial unrest hindered the intellectual legitimacy of these programs. The creation of Afro-American studies programs was often criticized because of its extraintellectual origins. During the decades following the demise of 1960s-style mass black political protests, American academia retreated on its commitment to Afro-American studies. There are decidedly fewer African American studies programs on college campuses today than there were thirty years ago. Many of the programs that have survived do so with drastically reduced resources.

Without the necessary empirical data, it is impossible to determine whether the decline of black studies programs/departments coincided with the increased diffusion of black scholars and black scholarly subjects throughout the existent disciplines. I suspect this was not the case, given the very limited racial diversity of faculty and curricula on most predominantly white campuses. It seems more likely that because of the decline in Afro-American pressure politics since the 1960s, American academia recognized and acted on its opportunity to assault an arena of study that it had never intended to fully support. At the very least, one must question the degree to which American academia was ever committed to institutionalizing the study of black peoples within its core curriculum.

The late 1970s saw not only a cadre of white graduate students emerging who would study race relations and black life and culture but also younger black scholars. By the late 1970s, a significant number of black graduate students, many of whom had attended predominantly white undergraduate colleges, bypassed black colleges when seeking employment and pursued assistant professorships at predominantly white colleges and universities. More than a few of these people never considered teaching at a predominantly black institution. Du Bois had not lived to see the era when young black scholars expected to be employed in predominantly white institutions.

Cultural racism, a variant of racism that does not pretend to be premised on scientific proof of black genetic inferiority, continues to thrive in the United States but in a less vehement and vicious manner than it did at the time of *The Souls of Black Folk*. Black American life continues to be devalued. For instance, there is weak white popular support for those public policies that are viewed as disproportionately benefiting blacks. The popular designation of black women as "welfare queens" (regardless of their impoverished economic condition) has been crucial in undermining mass public support for social welfare.[96] Similarly, it may now be politically problematic for the Congress or the president to generate a national urban policy (e.g., rebuilding urban infrastructures) because many whites do not perceive a self-interest in using their tax dollars in this manner. Whites who are disproportionately housed in suburbia increasingly view cities as minority enclaves. As a result, the black poor continue to be excluded from the implicit American social contract. Their suffering tends to lie outside the realm of white American empathy and moral concern.

Numerous contemporary black intellectuals, public and academic, attempt to confront the marginalization of blacks, particularly the black poor, within American society. In so doing, they embrace the legacy of W. E. B. Du Bois. At any rate, it appears that the efforts of these black intellectuals have had very little impact on the contemporary national mood. Those black intellectuals who champion the black poor are not institutionally situated in positions within the media that would allow them to be opinion shapers. Those black intellectuals who are sufficiently institutionalized within mainstream American media tend to be uncritical, establishment-status-seeking, "make-no-waves-on-the-race-question" type of Negroes like Mark Whittaker, contemporary editor in chief of *Newsweek* magazine. Curiously, at the very moment that blacks as a group cannot obtain sympathetic policy consideration from many whites, numerous individual blacks have been quite successful at generating public acceptance from whites. Consider the cases of entertainers such as Bill Cosby and Oprah Winfrey and politicians such as Colin Powell. The prominence and popularity of black public intellectuals such as bell hooks, Michael Eric Dyson, and Cornel West expanded at the same time that the needs of the group they are identified with are increasingly ignored. How does one assess the significance of black public intellectuals who have enormous visibility but little social and cultural influence?

Relevancy Angst or the "Utilitarian Imperative"[97]

The quest to be relevant to the needs of the black mass public is both cause and effect of a resilient and sometimes pernicious utilitarian imperative within Afro-American intellectual life.[98] This utilitarian imperative has been central to various popular educational philosophies that have taken root within black America following the demise of slavery. Given the dire plight of the majority of black Americans during the one hundred years following the end of slavery, it is understandable that blacks would evolve an approach to education that valued it primarily as a means of economically uplifting the individual, his or her family, or the ethnic group at large.

In much the same way, poorer Americans today either attend school in order to get a better-paying job or drop out of school if they do not perceive schooling as economically beneficial. Lost in this equation of education-for-upward-mobility is the possibility of education as a vehicle for critical enlightenment. For most post-antebellum blacks, education as illumination was deemed to be a luxury associated with bourgeois whiteness. For blacks, education must be useful and usefulness meant that education should somehow translate into improved material existences. Before one could contemplate the nature of good and evil, one had to eat! Unfortunately, the utilitarian ethos governing black educational philosophies also thoroughly influenced black intellectual life. As a result, a great deal of creativity was and continues to be stifled. If black thinkers had to prove their usefulness to the black freedom quest, they had to sacrifice certain intellectual or artistic interests that were not related to race advancement. How could one justify spending a lifetime studying Spinoza when so many black Americans were unable to meet the bare material necessities of life?

Concerning the utilitarian imperative in Afro-American intellectual life, Cornel West has written:

> The state of siege raging in the black community requires that black intellectuals accent the practical dimension of their work.... The accentuation of the practical dimension holds for most black intellectuals regardless of ideological persuasion—even more than for the stereotypical, pragmatic American intellectual. This is so not simply because of the power-seeking lifestyles and status-oriented dispositions of many black intellectuals, but also because of their relatively small number, which forces them to play multiple roles vis-à-vis the black community and, in addition, intensifies their need for self-vindication—the attempt

to justify to themselves that, given such unique opportunities and privileges, they are spending their time as they ought—which often results in activistic and pragmatic interests.[99]

Booker T. Washington took this utilitarian educational philosophy to its logical conclusion.[100] In his mind, blacks should be educated to increase their economic usefulness to a southern economic order that denied blacks equality. Following in the footsteps of his Hampton mentor, General Samuel Armstrong, Washington believed that blacks should be educated to become both economically self-sufficient and politically accepting of their inferiority to white southerners.[101] He chided blacks who were educated in ways that did not alleviate their economic impoverishment. Of what benefit was it to a black Alabaman in 1900 to be able to quote "Ode to a Grecian Urn"? In *Up From Slavery,* Washington had written: "One of the saddest things that I saw ... was a young man, who had attended some high school, sitting down in a one-room cabin, with grease on his clothing, filth all around him, and weeds in the yard and garden, engaged in studying a French grammar."[102]

In Washington's mind, such a man was utterly ludicrous. The Wizard of Tuskegee could not entertain the possibility that the man in greasy clothes realized aesthetic pleasure from learning French, or worse, that the benefit of learning French was in his mind a worthy trade-off for clean clothes and a weeded garden. He would have rather seen that man trained in some manner that rendered him a subservient exploited laborer for some white-owned business.

Ironically, Washington's ideological pronouncements about the need for industrial education for blacks helped to generate support for Tuskegee throughout the United States. However, in reality, Tuskegee was not primarily training an industrial workforce. Like Armstrong's Hampton, the primary mission of Tuskegee was to train normal schoolteachers who would either teach in existing schools or establish schools that advocated black acceptance of an inferior status in the South. Washington used Tuskegee to train teachers who would reside in black communities throughout the South and teach blacks to refrain from political involvement. Students at Tuskegee were forced to work as part of their studies but only to enhance their ideological commitment to the virtues of laboring. In effect, Tuskegee was a school for the ideological indoctrination of black advocates of white supremacy.[103]

Though decidedly different from Washington's, Du Bois's educational philosophy remained imprisoned in the utilitarian. Whereas Washington desired to educate the talented tenth to advocate black acceptance of the existent southern racial economic order, Du Bois promoted the belief that some blacks be given a classical liberal arts education, which in turn would generate in them dissatisfaction with the American racial order. Du Bois believed that a liberal arts education was crucial to the development of sensibilities that could educate and lead Negroes in the struggle for full citizenship rights. Negroes educated in such a fashion would understand the higher purposes of life and recognize the degree to which racism denied blacks the chance to realize their historical destiny. In effect, Du Bois defended liberal arts education on the grounds that it produced enlightened race leadership, a leadership that was necessary to direct the efforts of the black masses. Though Booker T. Washington and his Tuskegee agenda were championed by wealthy white northern industrialists, Washington was never able to silence all black criticism of his agenda. The two men had different normative conceptions of American race relations and the particular roles that educated blacks would play in pursuing this normative ideal. Du Bois believed in the possibility of racial equality. Washington did not.

Notes

Chapter 1

1. Luther Keith, "NAACP Speaker Gives Straight Talk on Racism," *Detroit News*, May 1, 2003. Also see Orlandar Brand-Williams, "Scholar at Freedom Fund Event," *Detroit News*, April 16, 2003; and Orlandar Brand-Williams, "NAACP Should Broaden Reach, Activist Says," *Detroit News*, April 28, 2003.

2. Manning Marable, W.E.B. *Du Bois: Black Radical Democrat* (Boston: Twayne Publishers, 1986), 214.

3. "The Souls of Black Folk: 100 Years Later" (brochure celebrating the Forty-Eighth Annual Freedom Fund Dinner, Detroit, MI, April 27, 2003).

4. Other significant conferences or public programs devoted to *The Souls of Black Folk* were sponsored by the University of Wisconsin–Madison, Oberlin College, University of Virginia, University of North Carolina, University of California–Riverside, and Miami University of Ohio. See "UC Riverside Celebrates Centennial of 'Souls of Black Folk,'" University of California–Riverside news release, April 23, 2003, www.newsroom.ucr. edu; Deborah Kong, "100 Years After Publication, 'Souls of Black Folk' Resonates," distributed by the Associated Press, April 22, 2003, www.zwire. com/site/news; and Lynne Duke, "A Searing Century for the Black Soul," *Washington Post*, April 27, 2003.

5. Felicia R. Lee, "A Challenge to White Supremacy, 100 Years Later; Scholars Revisit W. E. B. Du Bois, Who Found a New Way to Think About Race in America," *New York Times*, April 15, 2003.

6. "*The Souls of Black Folk* in the 21st Century" (Public Symposium, New York Historical Society, October 17–18, 2003).

7. Beth Potier, "'The Souls of Black Folk': Du Bois Institute Commemorates Centenary of Namesake's Landmark Work with Readings, Songs," *Harvard Gazette*, May 1, 2003, http://www.news.harvard.edu/ gazette/2003/05.01/09-souls.html.

8. Anica Butler, "Dual-Identity Perspective of 'Black Folk' Still Relevant," *Hartford Courant*, February 16, 2003.

9. Duke, "A Searing Century for the Black Soul."

10. Lee, "A Challenge to White Supremacy, 100 Years Later."

11. Ron Wynn, "Du Bois' Accomplishments Deserve to Be Emphasized," *Nashville City Paper*, April 29, 2003.

12. David Levering Lewis, *W.E.B. Du Bois: The Fight for Equality and the American Century, 1919–1963* (New York: Henry Holt and Company, 2001), 569.

13. "Tribute to W. E. B. Du Bois' *Souls of Black Folk*," *Tavis Smiley Show,* aired April 17, 2003, National Public Radio. Available on http://web.lexis-nexis.com.

14. John Bloom, "Assignment America: 'Souls of Black Folk,'" United Press International, April 25, 2003. Available on http://web.lexis-nexis.com. In this muddled, poorly written essay, Bloom questions whether Du Bois, who was so knowledgeable about "the great ideas of the West," could "really become a citizen of Ghana in his heart? ... Did he cast aside all these things for a fierce 'back to Africa' black separatism? Did he come to believe that America could be America without her Negro people?" Bloom in effect merges Du Bois with Marcus Garvey.

15. Duke, "A Searing Century for the Black Soul."

16. Lee, "A Challenge to White Supremacy."

17. Jim Auchmutey, "Remembering W. E. B. Du Bois," *Atlanta Journal and Constitution,* April 20, 2003.

18. Stuart Hall, "Tearing Down the Veil," *Guardian* (London), February 22, 2003.

19. James Weldon Johnson, *Along This Way* (New York: Viking, 1935), 203.

20. Farah Jasmine Griffin, "Introduction," in W. E. B. Du Bois, *The Souls of Black Folk* (New York: Barnes and Noble Classics, 2003), xx.

21. W. E. B. Du Bois, "Jefferson Davis as a Representative of Civilization," commencement address, June 25, 1890, in Herbert Aptheker, ed., *Against Racism: Unpublished Essays, Papers, Addresses, 1887–1961* (Amherst: University of Massachusetts Press, 1985), 16–17.

22. See Francis L. Broderick, *W.E.B. Du Bois: Negro Leader in a Time of Crisis* (Stanford: Stanford University Press, 1959), 18.

23. Booker T. Washington, *Up From Slavery* (1901) in *Three Negro Classics* (New York: Avon, 1965), 146–50.

24. W. E. B. Du Bois to Booker T. Washington, September 24, 1895, in Herbert Aptheker, ed., *The Correspondence of W.E.B. Du Bois, Volume I, 1877–1934* (Amherst: University of Massachusetts Press, 1973), 39.

25. W. E. B. Du Bois, *Dusk of Dawn: An Essay toward an Autobiography of a Race Concept* (New York: Harcourt, Brace, 1940), 55.

26. Booker T. Washington to W. E. B. Du Bois, March 11, 1900, in Aptheker, ed., *Correspondence, vol. I,* 44.

27. Marable, *W.E.B. Du Bois,* 43–44.

28. W. E. B. Du Bois, "My Evolving Program for Negro Freedom," in Rayford W. Logan, ed., *What the Negro Wants* (Chapel Hill: University of North Carolina Press, 1944), 54.

29. August Meier, *Negro Thought in America, 1880–1915* (Ann Arbor: University of Michigan Press, 1963, 1980).

30. Broderick, *W.E.B. Du Bois*, 66.

31. Du Bois, *Dusk of Dawn*, 80.

32. Griffin, "Introduction," xvi–xvii.

33. Du Bois, *Dusk of Dawn*, 80.

34. Broderick, *W.E.B. Du Bois*, 65.

35. Du Bois, *The Souls of Black Folk*, 32.

36. "'Souls of Black Folk': A Great Book by a Great Scholar, Touching the Spiritual Life of Colored People," *Guardian* (Boston), vol. 2, no. 23 (April 18, 1903), 1, 8.

37. "The Negro Question," *New York Times* (Saturday Review of Books and Art), April 24, 1903.

38. Broderick, *W.E.B. Du Bois*, 70; and Elliot M. Rudwick, *W.E.B. Du Bois, A Study in Minority Group Leadership* (Philadelphia: University of Pennsylvania Press, 1960), 69–70.

39. "Two Typical Leaders," *Outlook* (New York), vol. 73, no. 4 (May 23, 1903), 214–16. The *Outlook* warned its black readers "not [to] think about your woes or your wrongs. Meditate not on 'the souls of black folk,' but on 'the future of the American negro.' Look out, not in; forward, not backward. . . . Do not look long on the one-roomed cabins, or on the mortgaged farms, or the usurious rates of interest, or on the Jim Crow cars, or on the short-term schools" (216).

40. The Editor (John Spencer Basset), "Two Negro Leaders," *South Atlantic Quarterly*, vol. 2, no. 3 (July 1903), 267–72. Basset also observed that African Americans "are very weak human beings," and a "child race. To give them at once the liberty of adults would debauch them" (268).

41. "Social, Economic and Political Problems," *The American Monthly Review of Reviews*, vol. 38, no. 2 (August 1903), 249.

42. Theophilus Bolden Steward, "*The Souls of Black Folk*: Essays and Sketches," *American Journal of Sociology*, vol. 9, no. 1 (July 1903), 136–137.

43. "The Souls of Black Folk" (review), *Nation* (New York), vol. 76, no. 1980 (June 11, 1903), 481–82.

44. "Behind the Veil," *Congregationalist and Christian World* (Boston), vol. 888, no. 26 (June 27, 1903), 912.

45. "Politics, Economics, Sociology," *Independent* (New York), vol. 55, no. 2868 (November 19, 1903), 2746–48.

46. "How It Feels to Be a Problem," *Outwest* (Los Angeles), vol. 19, no. 1 (July 1903), 93.

47. "The Negro Problem," *Times Literary Supplement* (London), no. 88 (August 14, 1903), 243.

48. "Raymond," "Cultured Negro Model for Race," *Chicago Daily Tribune*, vol. 52, no. 143 (June 16, 1903), 1, 4.

49. Ida B. Wells-Barnett to W. E. B. Du Bois, May 30, 1903, in Aptheker, ed., *Correspondence, vol. I*, 54–56.

50. Ibid., Charles W. Chesnutt to W. E. B. Du Bois, June 27, 1903, 56–57.

51. Ibid., Casely Hayford to W. E. B. Du Bois, June 8, 1904, 75–76.
52. Ibid., Max Weber to W. E. B. Du Bois, March 30, 1905, 106–7.
53. Ibid., Jessie Fauset to W. E. B. Du Bois, December 26, 1903, 66.
54. W. E. B. Du Bois, "The Souls of Black Folk," *Independent,* vol. 57, no. 2920 (November 17, 1904), 1152.
55. W. E. B. Du Bois to Herbert Aptheker, January 7, 1949, in Herbert Aptheker, ed., *The Correspondence of W.E.B. Du Bois: Volume III, Selections, 1944–1963* (Amherst: University of Massachusetts Press, 1978), 257.
56. Lewis, *W.E.B. Du Bois,* 526–27.
57. W. E. B. Du Bois to Herbert Aptheker, February 27, 1953, in Aptheker, ed., *Correspondence, vol. III,* 343.
58. Ibid., editor's note by Herbert Aptheker, 344.
59. Lewis, *W.E.B. Du Bois,* 557, 561. Aptheker's version of the publication of the *Autobiography* is somewhat different from Lewis's. In 1958–1959 Du Bois wrote the basic draft of the *Autobiography,* and he revised the manuscript in 1960, according to Aptheker. Du Bois took the manuscript with him to Ghana in December 1961. Lewis asserts that the Soviet translator Vasily Kuznetsov translated the manuscript into Russian, and that the *Autobiography* appeared in the Soviet Union in 1962. Aptheker writes that the *Autobiography* was "published, in somewhat shortened versions, in 1964 and 1965, in China, the USSR, and the German Democratic Republic. Rescued from Accra, after the military coup of early 1966," Aptheker explains, the manuscript made its way to the United States and was printed "in the language of its composition in 1968." See Herbert Aptheker's "Editor's Preface," in W. E. B. Du Bois, *The Autobiography of W.E.B. Du Bois* (New York: International Publishers, 1968), 5.
60. Marable, *W.E.B. Du Bois,* 217.

Chapter 2

This chapter is a revision of a paper presented at the American Sociological Association Annual Meeting in Atlanta, Georgia, in August 2003. I want to thank Alford Young, Jr., and Charles Lemert for organizing this session and inviting me to participate. The original plan at the time of the invitation was to focus my comments about Black women from a careful reading of W. E. B. Du Bois's *The American Negro Family.* Published by Atlanta University Press in 1908, *The American Negro Family* is an important part of the Du Bois legacy but not a great source for discussing critical issues for Black women. I modified the assignment since I really welcomed the challenge of looking at W. E. B. Du Bois's legacy and the vision of Black women in sociology. My original title was "*The American Negro Family* and the Souls of Black Women," but I changed it here to reflect the real purpose of the essay.

1. Cheryl Townsend Gilkes, "The Margin as the Center of a Theory of History: African-American Women, Social Change and the Sociology of W. E. B. Du Bois," in *W. E. B. Du Bois on Race and Culture*, ed. Bernard Bell, Emily Grosholz, and James B. Stewart (New York: Routledge, 1996), 134.

2. Clara Rodriguez, *Changing Race: Latinos, the Census, and the History of Ethnicity in the United States* (New York: New York University Press, 2000).

3. Gilkes, "The Margin as the Center," 122.

4. W. E. B. Du Bois, *The American Negro Family* (New York: New American Library, 1969 [1908]). *The American Negro Family* was not in my university library, but I did find an edition that was reissued by the New American Library in 1969, a time when many early texts in African American studies were reprinted.

5. Such scholarship was important in developing a Black sociological tradition, which is being reclaimed by contemporary scholars. In addition to recent biographies by David Levering Lewis (*W. E. B. Du Bois: Biography of a Race, 1868–1919* [New York: Henry Holt, 1993]; *W. E. B. Du Bois: The Fight for Equality and the American Century, 1919–1963* [New York: Henry Holt, 2000]), scholars have long admired Du Bois for his scholarly contributions and for having been a model of an activist academic (see Manning Marable, *W. E. B. Du Bois: Black Radical Democrat* [Boston: Twayne, 1986]). More recently, scholars are rethinking the work of Atlanta University and the lack of recognition for the sociological work Du Bois did there. Scholars like Earl Wright II ("Using the Master's Tools: The Atlanta Sociological Laboratory and American Sociology, 1986–1924," *Sociological Spectrum* 22 [2002]: 15–39) are seeking to correct the record of contributions to urban sociology and fieldwork methodology.

6. Du Bois, *The American Negro Family*, 9.

7. James McKee, *Sociology and the Race Problem* (Urbana: University of Illinois Press, 1993).

8. Donna R. Gabaccia, *Immigration and American Diversity: A Social and Cultural History* (Malden, Mass.: Blackwell, 2002), 125.

9. Cheryl Townsend Gilkes, "The Gift of W. E. B. Du Bois and *The Souls of Black Folk*: An American Sociologist and an American Sociology," paper presented at the Eastern Sociological Society Meeting, Philadelphia, March 2003, 33.

10. Patricia Morton, *Disfigured Images: The Historical Assault on Afro-American Women* (New York: Praeger, 1991), 71.

11. David Levering Lewis, ed., *W. E. B. Du Bois: A Reader* (New York: Henry Holt, 1995).

12. See Gilkes, "The Margin as the Center" and "The Gift of W. E. B. Du Bois"; Patricia Hill Collins, "Gender, Black Feminism, and Black Political

Economy," in "The Study of African American Problems: W. E. B. Du
Bois's Agenda Then and Now," ed. Elijah Anderson and Tukufu Zuberi,
special issue, *Annals of the American Academy of Political and Social
Sciences* 568 (2000): 41–53, and *Black Feminist Thought: Knowledge,
Consciousness and the Politics of Empowerment* (New York: Routledge,
2000); and Farah Jasmine Griffin, "Black Feminists and Du Bois: Respect-
ability, Protection, and Beyond," in "The Study of African American
Problems: W. E. B. Du Bois's Agenda Then and Now," ed. Elijah Anderson
and Tukufu Zuberi, special issue, *Annals of the American Academy of
Political and Social Sciences* 568 (2000): 28–40.

13. Gilkes, "The Gift of W. E. B. Du Bois."
14. Collins, "Gender, Black Feminism, and Black Political Economy," 42.
15. Gilkes, "The Margin as the Center," 112.
16. Lewis, *W. E. B. Du Bois,* 302.
17. Deborah Gray White, *Ain't I a Woman: Female Slaves in the Plantation South* (New York: Norton, 1985).
18. Darlene Clark Hine and Kathleen Thompson, *A Shining Thread
of Hope: The History of Black Women in America* (New York: Broadway
Books, 1998), 93.
19. Hine and Thompson, *A Shining Thread of Hope,* 96.
20. Lewis, *W. E. B. Du Bois,* 302.
21. Collins, *Black Feminist Thought;* Morton, *Disfigured Images.*
22. Lewis, *W. E. B. Du Bois,* 304.
23. Collins, *Black Feminist Thought,* 5.
24. Kenneth W. Goings, *Mammy and Uncle Mose* (Bloomington: Indiana
University Press, 1994); Morton, *Disfigured Images.*
25. Darlene Clark Hine, "Rape and the Inner Life of Black Women:
Thoughts on the Culture of Dissemblance," in *Hine Sight,* ed. Darlene Clark
Hine, 37–47 (Brooklyn, N.Y.: Carlson Publications, 1994).
26. Media representations in narrative films are directed at contemporary
audiences; therefore, these films are not interested in historical accuracy but
in creating fictions for the comfort of those audiences (Hernan Vera and
Andrew Gordon, *Screen Saviors: Hollywood Fictions of Whiteness.* Lanham, Md.: Rowman & Littlefield, 2003). However, these new images show
contemporary audiences that a Black woman had power and influence at
a time when little power would have been extended to her. It is interesting
that this screenplay was written by Tina Andrews, an African American.
She might want to retell this story showing a powerful Black woman, but
many audiences might see this representation as historically accurate.
27. John Dollard, *Caste and Class in a Southern Town* (Garden City,
N.Y.: Doubleday, 1957 [1949]); Morton, *Disfigured Images.*
28. Collins, *Black Feminist Thought;* Morton, *Disfigured Images.*
29. Lewis, *W. E. B. Du Bois,* 309.
30. Du Bois, *The American Negro Family,* 147.
31. Quoted in Lewis, *W. E. B. Du Bois,* 308.

32. Lewis, *W. E. B. Du Bois*, 309.

33. Lewis, *W. E. B. Du Bois*, 305.

34. Deborah Gray White, *Ain't I a Woman: Female Slaves in the Plantation South* (New York: Norton, 1985).

35. Deborah Gray White, *Too Heavy a Load: Black Women in Defense of Themselves, 1894–1994* (New York: Norton, 1999), 306.

36. Morton, *Disfigured Images*, 71.

37. Griffin, "Black Feminists and Du Bois," 34.

38. Stephanie Shaw, *What a Woman Ought to Be and Do: Black Professional Women During the Jim Crow Era* (Chicago: University of Chicago Press, 1996), 16.

39. Collins, *Black Feminist Thought*, 86.

40. W. E. B. Du Bois, *The Souls of Black Folk*, ed. Henry Louis Gates, Jr., and Terri Hume Oliver (New York: Norton, 1999 [1903]), 47.

41. Du Bois, *The Souls of Black Folk*, 47.

42. Du Bois, *The Souls of Black Folk*, 51.

43. Du Bois, *The Souls of Black Folk*, 51.

44. Du Bois, *The Souls of Black Folk*, 51.

45. Du Bois, *The Souls of Black Folk*, 51–52.

46. At Brandeis I gained an education for which I will be forever grateful, but I also had to do a lot of teaching at the same time. Like many other people of color in graduate school in the 1970s, I had to learn the new race scholarship on my own although Brandeis faculty were supportive and I really learned much about conducting research. Yet, most importantly, I had a place where I was given support to think about issues that were not in the mainstream. When I learned about other graduate programs, I realized the significance of the gift I had been given.

Chapter 3

1. In making his argument about what constituted Du Bois's early confrontation with the problematic of the African American experience, Holt focused his assessment of Du Bois's scholarship on five of his publications: (1) "The Study of Negro Problems," *Annals of the American Academy of Political and Social Science* 11 (January 1898): 1–23, often regarded as his prolegomenon for a sociology of black Americans; (2) "The Conservation of the Races," a paper delivered to the American Negro Academy in 1897 and first published in its Occasional Papers series (see Du Bois, "The Conservation of the Races," in *W. E. B. Du Bois: On Sociology and the Black Community*, ed. D. S. Green and E. D. Driver, 238–49 [Chicago: University of Chicago Press, 1978]); (3) "The Negroes of Farmville, Virginia: A Social Study," *Bulletin of the Department of Labor* 14 (January 1898): 138, also in *W. E. B. Du Bois: On Sociology and the Black Community*, ed. Green and Driver, 165–96; (4) *The Philadelphia Negro*:

A Social Study (Philadelphia: University of Pennsylvania Press, 1996 [1899]); and (5) *The Souls of Black Folk* (Boulder, Colo.: Paradigm Publishers, 2004 [1903]). Thomas Holt, "W. E. B. Du Bois's Archeology of Race: Re-Reading 'The Conservation of Race,'" in *W. E. B. Du Bois, Race, and the City: The Philadelphia Negro and Its Legacy*, ed. Thomas J. Sugrue and Michael B. Katz (Philadelphia: University of Pennsylvania Press, 1998).

However, in accounting for all of Du Bois's major work during the turn toward the twentieth century, it is possible to reclassify Holt's framework along theoretical, empirical, and methodological points of consideration. In doing so, this early phase of Du Bois's scholarly career can be categorized as an effort to:

- ascertain the meaningfulness of race as a social category. For the theoretical dimension, compare "The Conservation of Race" and *The Souls of Black Folk*;
- document the barriers and obstacles inhibiting the social advancement of African Americans, and define some strategies and ideas for resolving them. For the empirical dimension, compare "The Striving of the Negro People," *Atlantic Monthly* 80 (August 1897): 194–98; "The Study of Negro Problems"; "The Negroes of Farmville, Virginia"; *The Philadelphia Negro*; "The Negro in the Black Belt: Some Social Sketches," *Bulletin of the Department of Labor* 4 (May 1899): 401–17; "The Talented Tenth," in *The Negro Problem: A Series of Articles by Representative American Negroes of Today*, ed. Booker T. Washington (New York: James Pott, 1904); "The Future of the Negro Race in America," *East and West* 2 (January 1904): 4–19; "The Economic Future of the Negro," *Publication of the American Economics Association* 7 (February 1906): 219–42; "Reconstruction and Its Benefits," *American Historical Review* 15 (July 1910): 781–99; or
- illustrate how historical analysis, demographic data, fieldwork, and survey research can be employed to further prior objectives. For the methodological dimension, compare "The Suppression of the African Slave Trade to the United States of America, 1683–1870" (Cambridge, Mass.: Harvard Historical Studies I, 1896); *The Philadelphia Negro*; "The Negroes of Farmville, Virginia"; "The Twelfth Census and the Negro Problems," *Southern Workman* 29 (January 1900): 30–59; *The Black North in 1901: A Social Study* [Reprint] (New York: Arno Press, 1969 [1901]); "The Problem of Housing the Negro," *Southern Workman* 30 (July–December 1901): 390–95, 486–93, 535–42, 601–4, 688–93; "The Laboratory in Sociology at Atlanta University," *Annals of the American Academy of Political and Social Science* 21 (May 1903): 16–63.

2. See Henry Louis Gates and Terri Hume Oliver, eds., *The Souls of Black Folk: W. E. B. Du Bois* (New York: Norton, 1994); Charles Lemert, "Foreword: The Cultured Souls of W. E. B. Du Bois," in *The Souls of Black Folk* (Boulder, Colo.: Paradigm Publishers, 2004); David Levering Lewis, *W. E. B. Du Bois: Biography of a Race* (New York: Henry Holt, 1993); Tommy Lott, "Du Bois and Locke on the Scientific Study of the Negro," *Boundary* 27, no. 3 (2000): 135–52; Cynthia D. Schrager, "Both Sides of the Veil: Race, Science, and Mysticism in W. E. B. Du Bois," *American Quarterly* 48, no. 4 (1996): 551–86; Adolph Reed, *W. E. B. Du Bois and American Political Thought: Fabianism and the Color Line* (New York: Oxford University Press, 1997); Shamoon Zamir, *Dark Voices* (Chicago: University of Chicago Press, 1995).

This vision of Du Bois's scholarly profile is also evident in discussions about Du Bois's

- contribution to racial theory; see Anthony Appiah, "The Uncompleted Argument: Du Bois and the Illusions of Race," in *Race, Writing, and Difference,* ed. Henry Louis Gates, Jr. (Chicago: University of Chicago Press, 1986); S. Brodwin, "The Veil Transcended: Form and Meaning in W. E. B. Du Bois' *The Souls of Black Folk,*" *Journal of Black Studies* 2 (March 1972): 303–21; S. C. Gilman, "The Color Line and Humanism: An Ethical Study of W. E. B. Du Bois," *Journal of Human Relations* 20 (1972): 397–415; Thomas Holt, "The Political Use of Alienation: W. E. B. Du Bois on Politics, Race, and Culture," *American Quarterly* 42, no. 2 (1990): 100–115; W. Moses, "W. E. B. Du Bois' 'The Conservation of Races' and Its Context: Idealism, Conservatism, and Hero Worship," *Massachusetts Review* 34, no. 2 (1993): 275–94; Kenneth Mostern, "Three Theories of the Race of W. E. B. Du Bois," *Cultural Critique* (Fall 1996): 27–63; Ross Posnock, *Color and Culture: Black Writers and the Making of the Modern Intellectual* (Cambridge, Mass.: Harvard University Press, 1998); Arnold Rampersad, *The Art and Imagination of W. E. B. Du Bois* (New York: Schocken, 1976); Schrager, "Both Sides of the Veil"; Zamir, *Dark Voices;*
- vision of the relationship of scholarship to public affairs; see F. L. Broderick, "The Academic Training of W. E. B. Du Bois," *Journal of Negro Education* 27 (Winter 1958): 10–16, and "German Influences on the Scholarship of W. E. B. Du Bois," *Phylon* 19 (Winter 1958): 367–71; J. De Marco, *The Social Thought of W. E. B. Du Bois* (Lanham, Md.: University Press of America, 1983); Elliot Rudwick, "W. E. B. Du Bois and the Atlanta University Studies of the Negro," *Journal of Negro Education* 26 (1957): 466, and *W. E. B. Du Bois: Propagandist of the Negro Protest* (New York: Atheneum, 1969); and W. J. Lange, "W. E. B. Du Bois and the First Scientific Study of Afro-America," *Phylon* 44 (1983); and

- relationship to twentieth-century American social thought; see H. C. La Rue, "W. E. B. Du Bois and the Pragmatic Method of Truth," *Journal of Human Relations* 19 (1971): 82–96; August Meier, *Negro Thought in America, 1880–1915* (Ann Arbor: University of Michigan Press, 1966); Cornel West, *The American Evasion of Philosophy: A Genealogy of Pragmatism* (Madison: University of Wisconsin Press, 1990).

Moreover, this understanding has been addressed

- in biographies of him; see Broderick, "W. E. B. Du Bois: History of an Intellectual," in *Black Sociologists: Historical and Contemporary Perspectives,* ed. James E. Blackwell and Morris Janowitz, 324 (Chicago: University of Chicago Press, 1974); Dan S. Green and Edwin D. Driver, "Introduction," in *W. E. B. Du Bois: On Sociology and the Black Community,* ed. Dan S. Green and Edwin D. Driver (Chicago: University of Chicago Press, 1978); V. Hamilton, *W. E. B. Du Bois: A Biography* (New York: Crowell, 1972); L. A. Lacy, *Cheer the Lonesome Traveler: The Life of W. E. B. Du Bois* (New York: Dell, 1972); Manning Marable, *W. E. B. Du Bois: Black Radical Democrat* (Boston: Twayne, 1986); J. B. Moore, *W. E. B. Du Bois* (Boston: Twayne, 1981);
- in anthologies on varied aspects of his life and work; see John Bracey, August Meier, and Elliott Rudwick, *The Black Sociologist: The First Half Century* (Belmont, Calif.: Wadsworth, 1971); "W. E. B. Du Bois Memorial Issue," *Freedomways* 1 (1965); R. W. Logan, ed., *W. E. B. Du Bois: A Profile* (New York: Hill & Wang, 1971);
- in intellectual histories of African American social thought at the dawn of the twentieth century; see Bracey, Meier, and Rudwick, *The Black Sociologist;* S. Fullinwider, *The Mind and Mood of Black America* (Homewood, Ill.: Dorsey Press, 1969); Kevin K. Gaines, *Uplifting the Race: Black Leadership, Politics, and Culture in the Twentieth Century* (Princeton, N.J.: Princeton University Press, 1996); Green and Driver, "Introduction"; Rampersad, *The Art and Imagination of W. E. B. Du Bois;* Reed, *W. E. B. Du Bois and American Political Thought;* Sugrue and Katz, *W. E. B. Du Bois, Race, and the City.*

3.   Thinking of Du Bois's work in this way poses a challenge to scholars who have striven to place Du Bois's scholarship firmly within disciplinary boundaries such as sociology, history, and political science. Clearly, admirable efforts have been undertaken by scholars to situate Du Bois's relevance to particular academic disciplines (Marable, *W. E. B. Du Bois: Black Radical Democrat;* Rampersad, *The Art and Imagination of W. E. B. Du Bois;* Reed, *W. E. B. Du Bois and American Political Thought*). Perhaps the best case of this is in the discipline of sociology, where numerous scholars have tried to claim him as a disciple of this discipline precisely because he wrote so much

about the role that sociology could play in transforming public understanding of the social conditions affecting African American life (Green and Driver, "Introduction"). However, even a casual review of Du Bois's scholarship makes clear that his aims and ideas concerning scholarship escape simple depiction as relevant to a particular academic discipline above and beyond others. For instance, one can think of a sociologist's disclaiming or completely ignoring Du Bois's more literary-style products, such as his novel *Dark Princess* (Millwood, N.Y.. Kraus-Thomson Organization, 1974 [1928]) or even sections and chapters of *The Souls of Black Folk*, which may seem in style and tone to be more suited to the humanities than to social science. Alternatively, humanist scholars may have less regard for *The Philadelphia Negro* or any of Du Bois's empirical studies of the social conditions affecting African Americans if the objective of those scholars is to locate Du Bois in some canon of humanistically centered theorizing about race. The effort to firmly embed Du Bois in one or another academic discipline risks neglecting or diminishing recognition of some of his scholarly contributions that may not appear to be relevant to the empirical or epistemological orientation of the particular discipline but that may inform about his overarching scholarly agenda.

4. Having said this, it would be foolish to argue that Du Bois's thoughts did not mature over time. Indeed, the evidence for this maturation resides in Du Bois's having moved across various schools of thinking, from his early infatuation with German idealism and American pragmatism to an extreme commitment to Marxism in his effort to define and pose solutions to the "Negro Problem." However, it would be equally foolish to argue that each of his works offered only a mere twist of novelty in exposing its readership to vastly underexplored and erroneously conceptualized questions concerning race and black Americans. After all, many of his works have become classics in African American social thought because each offers a different methodological or epistemological approach toward investigating the experiences of African Americans, or otherwise poses reconsiderations of problems in light of changing historical circumstances. Accordingly, a more appropriate stance toward his work would acknowledge that the corpus of his scholarship centers on an ambitious and intriguing effort to raise and answer the questions presented by Thomas Holt from diverse intellectual standpoints. More importantly, he strove to revisit and, when necessary, redefine his claims in light of new evidence or deeper exploration of various schools of thought.

5. In fact, the first chapter of *Souls*, "Of Our Spiritual Strivings," is a revisitation of the paper "Strivings of the Negro People," which was published in the popular periodical *Atlantic Monthly* in 1897, prior to the publication of *Negro*. Moreover, other ideas and arguments in *Souls* had their genesis in publications produced prior to *Negro* (Lewis, *W. E. B. Du Bois*).

6. In making this claim I stand with others (e.g., Holt, "W. E. B. Du Bois's Archeology of Race"; Lemert, "Foreword: The Cultured Souls of

W. E. B. Du Bois") who have asserted that rather than regarding each work as distant from the other—*Negro* moving toward formal social science and *Souls* toward the humanities—each is actually in conversation with the other on matters of method and analysis.

7. Arguments about the overlapping objectives of *Negro* and *Souls* have been alluded to by Ernest Allen, Jr., "Du Boisian Double Consciousness: The Unsustainable Argument," *The Black Scholar* 33, no. 2 (2003): 25–43; Schrager, "Both Sides of the Veil"; and Zamir, *Dark Voices*. Yet, in comparison to my argument, each of these individuals chose to explore a different point of significance about the matter, mostly by focusing on the intentions and outcomes of *Souls* for advancing Du Bois's intellectual and political agenda.

8. Du Bois, *Dusk of Dawn: An Essay toward An Autobiography of a Concept* (New York: Schocken Books, 1968 [1940]).

9. Lewis, *W. E. B. Du Bois*. Mostern ("Three Theories of the Race of W. E. B. Du Bois") argues that Du Bois's personal tribulations with race throughout his life correspond with a threefold manner in which he wrote about the topic (each phase of writing fitting into a specific, chronologically ordered phase of his life history). Mostern posits that the first is an individualist orientation, whereby Du Bois maintained that race was an identity construct foisted upon the individual by the external social world, thus circumscribing how the public read and reacted to individuals. The second phase is an essentialist orientation that suggests that people who are ascribed to a particular racial category function similarly in thought and action (thus re-creating a sense of racial culture and racial collectives). The third involves fostering a claim that the problematic of race must be overcome until race is no longer socially meaningful. Both the *Souls of Black Folk* and *The Philadelphia Negro* were produced during Du Bois's transition from the first to the second of these phases.

10. Broderick, "The Academic Training of W. E. B. Du Bois," and "German Influences"; Lewis, *W. E. B. Du Bois*.

11. An earlier work by Du Bois, "The Negroes of Farmville, Virginia," was in methodological design and argument a precursor to *The Philadelphia Negro,* and, thus, informed his efforts in conducting research in Philadelphia.

12. In presenting the material in this fashion, Du Bois followed through on the mandate for sociological inquiry that he presented in "The Study of Negro Problems," which called for mutual consideration of all four of these domains in order to construct a thorough investigation of the situation of African Americans. More is to follow on the issue of how satisfied Du Bois was with the claims that *Negro* made in association with that mandate.

13. Two rich synopses of the elitist overtones of *Negro* that also accurately capture the methodological and empirical fruits of Du Bois's work for this book are provided by Tukufu Zuberi, "W. E. B. Du Bois's Sociology: *The Philadelphia Negro* and Social Science," *Annals of the American Academy of Political and Social Science* 595 (September 2004): 146–56; and Reed, *W. E. B. Du Bois and*

American Political Thought. While highlighting the vast and varied research methodologies that Du Bois employed, both also emphasize Du Bois's overtly moralistic critical assessment of the African American poor and working classes (particularly by stressing Du Bois's claim that such people must commit to better cultural mores in order to advance in American society). Reed goes further by discussing how Du Bois's investment in empirical research in *Negro* is the introduction of a scientific-knowledge-for-the-remediation-of-social-problems logic that problematically positions intellectuals and scholars as social reform managers in a liberal technocratic civil society (which, for Reed, is what the United States is headed toward in the early twentieth century). Of course, what Du Bois delivers in his later, more explicitly Marxist-informed, scholarship indicates that he eventually aspired to pursue a more transformative and complex sociopolitical agenda pertaining to the advancement of African Americans than as represented by liberal technocratic interventionism.

14. Du Bois, *The Philadelphia Negro*, 1.

15. Zamir, *Dark Voices.*

16. Unfortunately, the contemporary significance of *Souls* often rests in references made to one or more of what have become a series of highly clichéd statements and concepts in the book. Some of the more common statements are "the problem of the twentieth century is the problem of the color line," and the reference to a double consciousness as a social psychological property of black Americans. Undoubtedly, Du Bois's claim about the problem of race in the twentieth century appears from a contemporary vantage point to be one of considerable vision and foresight, and references to the notion of the double consciousness has sparked extensive discussion about African American racial identity throughout modernity. However, it is also the case that intensive preoccupation with this clichéd terminology does little to capture the intricacies, depth, and implications of Du Bois's argument in *Souls,* including how that argument related to his broader intellectual and political objectives for black Americans at the turn toward the twentieth century.

17. Du Bois, *The Philadelphia Negro*, 2.

18. Du Bois, *The Philadelphia Negro*, 3.

19. Du Bois, *The Philadelphia Negro*, 3.

20. Du Bois, *The Philadelphia Negro*, 3.

21. The chapter by Jerry G. Watts in this volume provides a rich and provocative assessment of the scholarly and political implications of Du Bois's racial consciousness taking shape within such parameters, especially as they pertain to his producing *The Souls of Black Folk.*

22. In an insightful commentary about Du Bois's methodology, Schrager ("Both Sides of the Veil") argues that the claims made in *Negro* pose an immediate, yet vastly underrecognized, challenge to an emerging Victorian-era conviction that social scientists could operate as objective investigators armed with value-neutrality and dispassionate, objective outlooks on the social world.

23. Du Bois, *The Philadelphia Negro*, 269–89.

24. Du Bois, *The Philadelphia Negro*, 283–84.

25. Du Bois, *The Philadelphia Negro*, 284.

26. Du Bois, *The Philadelphia Negro*, 284.

27. Du Bois, *The Philadelphia Negro*, 145, 283–84.

28. The strong interpretive style in which he delivers his argument in *Negro* would be referred to by the mid-twentieth century as the authoritative ethnography; see Norman K. Denzin and Yvonna S. Lincoln, "Introduction: The Discipline and Practice of Qualitative Research," in *Handbook of Qualitative Resaerch*, 1–28 (Thousand Oaks, Calif.: Sage, 2000).

29. Du Bois, *The Philadelphia Negro*, 322.

30. Du Bois, *The Philadelphia Negro*, 350.

31. Du Bois, *The Philadelphia Negro*, 322–55.

32. Du Bois, *The Philadelphia Negro*, 322.

33. Du Bois, *The Philadelphia Negro*, 350.

34. Schrager, "Both Sides of the Veil."

35. Zamir, *Dark Voices*, 98.

36. Lott, "Du Bois and Locke," 136.

37. Zamir, *Dark Voices*, 97.

38. Zamir, *Dark Voices*, 98.

39. Du Bois, *The Souls of Black Folk*, 10–11.

40. Du Bois, *The Souls of Black Folk*, 11.

41. Du Bois, *The Souls of Black Folk*, 11.

42. Dickson D. Bruce, Jr., "W. E. B. Du Bois and the Idea of Double Consciousness," in *The Souls of Black Folk: W. E. B. Du Bois*, ed. Henry Louis Gates and Terri Hume Oliver, 236–44 (New York: Norton, 1999), 238.

43. Bruce, "W. E. B. Du Bois and the Idea of Double Consciousness," 238.

44. Bruce, "W. E. B. Du Bois and the Idea of Double Consciousness," 238.

45. Allen, "Du Boisian Double Consciousness," 30.

46. Aside from the work of Allen ("Du Boisian Double Consciousness") and the Watts chapter in this volume, some of the more intensive investigations of the intellectual foundations of Du Bois's concept of double consciousness have been explored by Robert Gooding-Williams, "Philosophy of History and Social Critique in *The Souls of Black Folk*," *Social Science Information* 26, no. 1 (1987): 99–114; Reed, *W. E. B. Du Bois and American Political Thought*; Schrager, "Both Sides of the Veil"; West, *The American Evasion of Philosophy*; Kirt H. Wilson, "Toward a Discursive Theory of Racial Identity: *The Souls of Black Folk* as a Response to Nineteenth-Century Biological Determinism," *Western Journal of Communication* 63, no. 2 (Spring 1999): 193–215; and Zamir, *Dark Voices*. While all agree that the term best reflects the existential position of more privileged African Americans, each offers distinct assessments of the extent to which the term was a product of that era's psychological or literary considerations of selfhood given Du Bois's exposure to psychologist William James at Harvard and readings of the literary figure Ralph

Waldo Emerson, who actually employed the term *double consciousness* (but for reasons far from Du Bois's own project concerning it). While the debate continues, points of consistency include how much the term was inspired by angst and anguish as central tenets in turn-toward-the-twentieth-century African American life, along with the varied forms of invisibility that African Americans encounter despite living in the midst of white Americans.

47. Allen, "Du Boisian Double Consciousness," 31.

48. Allen, "Du Boisian Double Consciousness." Indeed, Schrager goes so far as to say that double consciousness puts into the sociopolitical landscape the capacity for elite black Americans to maintain a "second sight" that allows for self-critique of political programs and policies because such African Americans are forced to become oriented toward second guessing and rethinking their social prospects. This logic overcomes the single-minded vision of individuals like Booker T. Washington who have committed to a narrow economic-uplift agenda without attentiveness to broad or deep issues of racial oppression that could stand in the way of such a platform ("Both Sides of the Veil," 574–575).

49. Other, more literary-style chapters in *Souls* also grapple with presenting the effects of color prejudice on black Americans in ways that formal social scientific analyses are incapable of doing. These chapters, including "Of the Quest of the Golden Fleece" and "Of the Coming of John," do the work of explaining the agonies and tensions of being a black American by presenting accounts of the pain and anguish experienced by fictional African American characters. *Souls* extends the work of *Negro* by pushing forward the question of what it feels like to occupy the social category of black American.

50. Du Bois, *The Souls of Black Folk*, 9.

51. Du Bois, *The Souls of Black Folk*, 2.

52. This claim has been offered by a range of contemporary scholars (Holt, "The Political Use of Alienation"; Schrager, "Both Sides of the Veil"; Wilson, "Toward a Discursive Theory of Racial Identity"; and Zamir, *Dark Voices*), some of whom have done so in order to counter Appiah's ("The Uncompleted Argument") highly acknowledged claim that Du Bois commits to racial essentialism in turn-toward-the-twentieth-century scholarship.

53. Wilson, "Toward a Discursive Theory of Racial Identity."

Chapter 4

1. Matthew Arnold, *Culture and Anarchy* (Cambridge: Cambridge University Press, 1961 [1869]), 69.

2. John Edgar Wideman, "Introduction," *The Souls of Black Folk* (New York: Vintage Books, 1990), ix–xvi.

3. Du Bois, *The Souls of Black Folk* (Boulder, Colo.: Paradigm Publishers, 2004), 2.

4. Du Bois, *The Souls of Black Folk*, vii.

5. Du Bois, *The Souls of Black Folk*, 1.

6. Du Bois, *The Souls of Black Folk*, 2.

7. For a defense of this claim, I fall back (with apologies for the self-reference) on myself. Charles Lemert, "The Race of Time: Deconstruction, Du Bois, and Reconstruction, 1873–1935," in *Dark Thoughts: Race and the Eclipse of Society* (New York: Routledge, 2002), 223–46.

8. Lemert, "The Race of Time," 113.

9. Frantz Fanon, *The Wretched of the Earth* (New York: Grove Press, 1968 [1963]), 222. Among those who overestimate the debt of Fanon to Du Bois is Sylvia Winter, "Towards the Sociogenic Principle: Fanon, Identity, the Puzzle of Conscious Experience, and What It Is Like to Be 'Black,'" in *National Identities and Sociopolitical Changes in Latin America,* ed. Mercedes F. Durán-Cogan and Antonio Gómez-Moriana (New York: Routledge, 2001), chap. 3.

10. Cornel West, "Cultural Politics of Difference," in *Out There: Marginalization and Contemporary Culture,* ed. Russell Ferguson, Martha Gever, Trinh T. Minh-Ha, and Cornel West (Cambridge: MIT Press, 1990), 19–20.

11. Harold Cruse, *The Crisis of the Negro Intellectual* (New York: Quill, 1984 [1967]), 110.

12. Jerry Gafio Watts, *Amiri Baraka: The Politics and Art of a Black Intellectual* (New York: New York University Press, 2001), 14.

13. Watts, *Amiri Baraka,* 20.

Chapter 5

1. Russell Jacoby, *The Last Intellectuals: American Culture in the Age of Academe* (New York: Farrar, Straus and Giroux, 1987).

2. For other critiques of the Jacoby book, see Bruce Robbins, ed., *Intellectuals: Aesthetics, Politics, Academics* (Minneapolis: University of Minnesota Press, 1990), xii–xvii. For a very perceptive review of Jacoby, see Barry W. Sarchett, "Russell Jacoby, Anti-Professionalism, and the Politics of Cultural Nostalgia," *The Minnesota Review,* no. 39 (Fall/Winter 1992/93): 122–42.

3. Perhaps Jacoby's racial parochialism should not have been surprising. He had been a graduate student of historian Christopher Lasch. Lasch had previously written a book about American intellectuals that ignored blacks. See Lasch, *The New Radicalism, 1889–1963: The Intellectual as Social Type* (New York: Knopf, 1965).

4. Note, for instance, the absence of a discussion of Du Bois in Dorothy Ross, *The Origins of American Social Science* (Cambridge: Cambridge University Press, 1991).

5. For a study of a prominent nineteenth-century Afro-American learned society, see Alfred A. Moss, Jr., *The American Negro Academy: Voice of the Talented Tenth* (Baton Rouge: Louisiana State University Press, 1981).

6. That lecture can be found in Alexander Crummell, *Destiny and Race: Selected Writings, 1840–1898*, ed. Wilson Jeremiah Moses (Amherst: University of Massachusetts Press, 1992), 289–300.

7. Ross Posnock, *Color and Culture: Black Writers and the Making of the Modern Intellectual* (Cambridge, Mass.: Harvard University Press, 1998).

8. Posnock's *Color and Culture* suffers from ahistoricism. He attempts to claim that Du Bois and others of his generation were cosmopolitan opponents of the logics of black ethnic/racial authenticity. But the substance of ethnic/racial authenticity that Posnock invokes does not become central to Afro-American thought until the 1960s and 1970s and cannot be understood without the histories of the civil rights movement and the black power era. It would not have made sense during the 1920s to have said to Du Bois or James Weldon Johnson that they were insufficiently "Negro." Neither Du Bois nor Johnson was confronted with anything resembling the idea of authenticity as it would become known in the 1970s or since.

Another more fundamental flaw in the Posnock book is that he reproduces aspects of the marginalization of black thinkers that he is supposedly intent on exposing. He continually tells the reader that Du Bois et al. were not recognized as cosmopolitan or as modern intellectuals. For instance, Posnock makes statements such as "One reason the cosmopolitanism found in say, Du Bois and Locke has never been appreciated is that they defamiliarize the word" (Posnock, *Color and Culture*, 10).

Needless to say, many black intellectuals appreciated the cosmopolitanism of Du Bois and Locke. Black intellectuals of the time had little doubt that Du Bois was an intellectual. Much of Posnock's entire thesis rests on the silencing of the thoughts of black intellectuals about other black intellectuals. He is only concerned with what white intellectuals thought about black intellectuals. This is a bizarre posture for a book that purports to be a revisionary discussion of Afro-American intellectuals.

9. For a commentary on Du Bois's patriarchal sensibilities concerning the ideal Negro intellectual, see Hazel V. Carby's *Race Men* (Cambridge, Mass.: Harvard University Press, 1998), chap. 1. While Carby is correct in pointing out Du Bois's sexist assumptions in *The Souls of Black Folk*, her critique is somewhat baffling insofar as she spends far too much energy describing the dismissal of Du Bois's sexism by contemporary Afro-American male intellectuals, particularly Cornel West.

10. While he does not address sexism in the thought of cosmopolitan Afro-American male intellectuals, Posnock includes Pauline Hopkins and Zora Neale Hurston in the ranks of the cosmopolitan.

11. Culturally parochial images of blacks are not monopolized by white Americans. One need only peruse *Ebony* magazine to see the black American valorization of entertainers, comedians, and athletes at the expense of

black thinkers. In *Ebony*'s annual survey of the hundred most influential black Americans, intellectuals are regularly underrepresented, if represented at all.

12. There are a few black political commentators that appear on national television but even they tend to rest among the second-tier commentators. These black figures, including Juan Williams, Alan Keyes, and Armstrong Williams, are as mundane and uninsightful as their white peers. One might erroneously conclude from this that the dominant criteria for visibility on corporate television media are mundaneness and mediocrity. However, if mundaneness and mediocrity were the sole determining criteria for employment as media gurus, we could not explain the overwhelming whiteness of the media commentators. After all, there are certainly numerous blacks who have earned their mediocrity bona fides and who are waiting for their days in the sun. Why are they not called up to the major leagues? In January 2005, news stories broke that Armstrong Williams was secretly paid by the Bush administration to propagate No Child Left Behind via his role as a news commentator. Williams had taken mediocrity to an entirely new level. For his efforts, he received payment of two hundred and forty thousand dollars. I would not be surprised if other well-known commentators were guilty of similar dishonest deeds.

13. For a very informative analysis of media depictions of black Americans, see Robert M. Entman and Andrew Rojecki, *The Black Image in the White Mind: Media and Race in America* (Chicago: University of Chicago Press, 2000).

14. To attain a sense of the vileness and pervasiveness of white antiblack racism at the turn of the century, see George M. Fredrickson, *The Black Image in the White Mind* (New York: Harper and Row, 1971); Thomas Gossett, *Race: The History of an Idea in America* (New York: Schocken Books, 1965); Joel Williamson, *The Crucible of Race: Black-White Relations in the American South since Emancipation* (New York: Oxford University Press, 1984); or Gary B. Nash and Richard Weiss, eds., *The Great Fear: Race in the Mind of America* (New York: Holt, Rinehart and Winston, 1970).

15. Posnock perceptively uses this term to refer to Phillis Wheatley in regard to the ways that she "exhibited." The young Frederick Douglass would become another racial exhibit. In effect, instead of engaging their writings and ideas, the very fact that they wrote and generated ideas turned them into deviant exoticized commodities masquerading as "curiosities." Similar cultural dynamics may have been at work in the white reception of the young Du Bois. See Posnock, *Color and Culture*, 51–53.

16. Roger Lane, *William Dorsey's Philadelphia and Ours: On the Past and Future of the Black City in America* (New York: Oxford University Press, 1991), 58.

17. See Roger Lane's *Roots of Violence in Black Philadelphia, 1860–1900* (Cambridge, Mass.: Harvard University Press, 1986). One of the most extensive efforts to document the scope of criminal activities within an expanding black northern urban ghetto at the turn of the century was

W. E. B. Du Bois's own *The Philadelphia Negro* (New York: Schocken, 1967 [1899]).

18. For a view of the class formations within the black community of Philadelphia at the end of the nineteenth century, see Roger Lane, *William Dorsey's Philadelphia and Ours*.

19. Kevin K. Gaines, *Uplifting the Race: Black Leadership, Politics, and Culture in the Twentieth Century* (Chapel Hill: University of North Carolina Press, 1996).

20. See entry on Francis James Grimke by Henry Warner Bowden in Henry Louis Gates, Jr., and Evelyn Brooks Higginbotham, eds., *African American Lives* (New York: Oxford University Press, 2004), 363–64.

21. See Dickson D. Bruce, Jr., *Archibald Grimke: Portrait of a Black Independent* (Baton Rouge: Louisiana State University Press, 1993).

22. Rayford W. Logan, *Howard University: The First Hundred Years, 1867–1967* (New York: New York University Press, 1969).

23. Kenneth R. Manning, *Black Apollo of Science: The Life of Ernest Everett Just* (New York: Oxford University Press, 1983).

24. August Meier and Elliott Rudwick, *Black History and the Historical Profession, 1915–1980* (Urbana: University of Illinois Press, 1986), 135.

25. David Levering Lewis, "Social Science, Ambition and Tuskegee," in *W. E. B. Du Bois: Biography of a Race, 1868–1919* (New York: Henry Holt, 1993), chap. 9, 211–37.

26. Atlanta University would also lose its land-grant appropriation from the state of Georgia in 1887 because it refused to segregate its dining halls. Black and white faculty ate together and with students in the dining hall. Black and white faculty lived alongside each other in university-owned housing. Such social fraternizing between the races was not allowed at Tuskegee.

For a discussion of the ways in which white foundations shaped black higher education in the direction of Booker T. Washington's plans, see William H. Watkins, *The White Architects of Black Education: Ideology and Power in America, 1865–1954* (New York: Teachers College Press, 2001).

27. On the Atlanta University Sociological Studies, see the following articles by Earl Wright, II: "The Atlanta Sociological Laboratory 1896–1924: A Historical Account of the First American School of Sociology," *The Western Journal of Black Studies* 26, no. 3 (2002): 165–74; "Using the Master's Tools: The Atlanta Sociological Laboratory and American Sociology, 1896–1924," *Sociological Spectrum* 22 (2002): 15–39; and "Why Black People Tend to Shout! An Earnest Attempt to Explain the Sociological Negation of the Atlanta Sociological Laboratory Despite Its Possible Unpleasantness," *Sociological Spectrum* 22 (2002): 335–61.

28. W. E. B. Du Bois, *The Atlanta University Publications* (Nos. 1, 2, 4, 8, 9, 11, 13, 14, 15, 16, 17, 18) (New York: Arno Press and the New York Times, 1968). Reprints of the above-listed individual Atlanta Studies were collected in one volume reprinted by Arno Press in 1968. Except for volumes 1 and 2, the Atlanta Studies were conceived and edited by Du Bois.

The Du Bois–edited volumes contained in the Arno Press collection are: vol. 4, *The Negro in Business* (1899); vol. 8, *The Negro Church* (1903); vol. 9, *Some Notes on Negro Crime Particularly in Georgia* (1904); vol. 11, *The Health and Physique of the Negro American* (1906); vol. 13, *The Negro American Family* (1908); vol. 14, *Efforts For Social Betterment among Negro Americans* (1910); vol. 15, *The College-Bred Negro American* (1910); vol. 16, *The Common School and the Negro American* (1911); vol. 17, *The Negro American Artisan* (1912); and vol. 18, *Morals and Manners among Negro Americans* (1914).

29. W. E. B. Du Bois, *Dusk of Dawn: An Essay Toward an Autobiography of a Race Concept* (New York: Schocken Books, 1968), 67–68.

30. In Du Bois's mind this meant engaging and using not only Western philosophy, literature, and art but also the newly developing social sciences.

31. Saunders Redding, "Introduction," W. E. B. Du Bois, *The Souls of Black Folk* (Greenwich, Ct.: Fawcett Publications, 1961), ix.

32. Amy Kaplan argues that in *Darkwater,* a volume of essays published almost two decades after *The Souls of Black Folk,* Du Bois would use the situation of Negroes in America as the vantage point to comment on the entirety of American and European civilizations. See Amy Kaplan, *The Anarchy of Empire in the Making of U.S. Culture* (Cambridge, Mass.: Harvard University Press, 2002), particularly "The Imperial Cartography of W. E. B. Du Bois," chap. 6.

33. Shamoon Zamir, *Dark Voices: W. E. B. Du Bois and American Thought, 1888–1903* (Chicago: University of Chicago Press, 1995), 137.

34. For a sampling of Douglass's writings, see William L. Andrews, ed., *The Oxford Frederick Douglass Reader* (New York: Oxford University Press, 1996). I have sometimes wondered if Douglass actually believed that America's professed ideals were its true ideals or if he claimed such beliefs as a rhetorical and political posture. After all, the existence of slavery and racism could not be treated as aberrations.

35. Du Bois's uncritical deference to Europe was present beginning in his undergraduate college years. In discussing his valorization of Bismarck during his days at Fisk, Du Bois states: "I did not understand at all, nor had my history courses led me to understand, anything of current European intrigue, of the expansion of European power into Africa ... of the fierce rivalry among white nations for controlling the profits from colonial raw material and labor—of all this I had no clear conception. I was blithely European and imperialist in outlook; democratic as democracy was conceived in America" (W. E. B. Du Bois, *Dusk of Dawn: An Essay Toward an Autobiography of a Race Concept* [New York: Schocken Books, 1968], 32).

36. According to David Levering Lewis, Du Bois traveled throughout Germany, Austria, Hungary, Italy, and parts of Poland during his graduate student days in Germany. He was not impressed with Poland, where he wit-

nessed crude class and racial prejudice (anti-Semitism). See Lewis, *W. E. B. Du Bois: Biography of a Race,* 127–49.

37. W. E. B. Du Bois, *The Souls of Black Folk,* 74. Charles Chesnutt, another bifurcated black intellectual, made comments similar to those of Du Bois. Like Du Bois, he found his material world constrained by the racial line but found escape in the freedom and acceptance of the world of ideas. Writing in his diary, Chesnutt stated: "What a blessing is literature.... Shut up in my study, without the companionship of one congenial mind, I can enjoy the society of the greatest wits and scholars ... [and] find myself in the company of the greatest men of earth." (The quote is reprinted in Posnock, *Color and Culture,* 14.)

38. Two of the most compelling discussions of the influence of Hegel on *The Souls of Black Folk* are Joel Williamson, *The Crucible of Race,* chap. 13; and Zamir, *Dark Voices,* particularly part 2.

39. In his history of American pragmatism, *The American Evasion of Philosophy: A Genealogy of Pragmatism,* Cornel West argues that Du Bois was a pragmatist. West also asserts that *The Souls of Black Folk* is steeped in pragmatism. West's argument in defense of this description of *Souls* is unconvincing. See Cornel West, *The American Evasion of Philosophy: A Genealogy of Pragmatism* (Madison: University of Wisconsin Press, 1989), 142–44. For a compelling critique of West's argument concerning pragmatism, Du Bois, and *Souls,* see Robert Gooding-Williams's review of the West text, "Evading Narrative Myth, Evading Prophetic Pragmatism: Cornel West's *The American Evasion of Philosophy,*" *Massachusetts Review* 32, no. 4 (Winter 1991): 517–43. Though he refutes the arguments of West, Gooding-Williams does not prove that Du Bois was free of pragmatism's influence. Williams merely shows that West has not proven this case. For a compelling argument in behalf of Du Bois as a pragmatist, see Posnock, *Color and Culture,* 111–45. Yet, even Posnock does not offer a compelling claim concerning pragmatism and *Souls.* It is possible that pragmatism had a tremendous influence on Du Bois's thinking throughout his long life without having been a guiding philosophy of *The Souls of Black Folk.*

40. Eric J. Sundquist, *To Wake the Nations: Race in the Making of American Literature* (Cambridge, Mass.: Harvard University Press, 1993), 457–539. Sundquist offers a discussion of the potential reasons why Du Bois chose to associate certain spirituals with certain chapters. *To Wake the Nations* offers, to my knowledge, the most extensive discussion of the varied meanings of Du Bois's use of the sorrow songs in *The Souls of Black Folk.*

41. Christopher A. Brooks, "The 'Musical' Souls of Black Folk: Can a Double Consciousness Be Heard?" in *The Souls of Black Folk: One Hundred Years Later,* ed. Dolan Hubbard (Columbia: University of Missouri Press, 2003), 278–79.

42. Lewis, *W. E. B. Du Bois: Biography of a Race,* 278.

43. See John Edgar Wideman, "Introduction," *The Souls of Black Folk* (New York: Vintage Books, 1990). On page xv, Wideman wrote: "In some quiet part of myself—a place where I first learned forty years ago, in the AME Zion church, versions of what Du Bois called—"Sorrow Songs," versions still sung today.

44. Herein I think that Cornel West, among others who argue that Martin Luther King, Jr., was an organic leader, is mistaken in his unwillingness to recognize that all publicly recognized leaders are deemed leaders because they differentiate themselves from the masses they are leading. Moreover, it is not clear that a charismatic leader like King could ever be organic to the masses of his followers. The charismatic connection is a distancing mechanism.

45. According to historian Henry May, "the culture to which Du Bois demanded admission, that in which he found solace, was the culture of the most conservative custodians, and the way he talked about it was the way that was soon to be rejected."

Furthermore, May notes in *The End of American Innocence: A Study of the First Years of Our Time, 1912–1917* (Chicago: Quadrangle Books, 1964), 87–88:

> Neither Washington nor Du Bois could possibly have guessed what bucket to cast down or where to cast it. Jazz, despised by serious Negroes, was already blooming in New Orleans dives and, in St. Louis, W. C. Handy was publishing his great blues. The Negro was to have a bigger part in the coming change in American culture than he had ever had in any American cultural movement before. Not through admission to the realm of polite letters but its overthrow Negroes were to win money, world-wide fame, enthusiastic white imitation, and even, in the long run, some solid steps toward real equality.

46. Houston A. Baker, Jr., *Long Black Song: Essays in Black American Literature and Culture* (Charlottesville: University Press of Virginia, 1972), 97. The quote is from Matthew Arnold, *Culture and Anarchy,* ed. J. Dover Wilson (Cambridge: Cambridge University Press, 1963), 48, 70.

47. Baker, *Long Black Song,* 97.

48. Du Bois, *The Souls of Black Folk,* 6.

49. Concerning Du Bois's ambivalence about his linkages to "black folk," see Zamir, *Dark Voices,* 138–39 and 142–43.

50. Du Bois, *The Philadelphia Negro,* 310–18, and Zamir, *Dark Voices,* 148–49.

51. Posnock, *Color and Culture,* 111.

52. For a discussion of Du Bois's engagement with the thought of Emerson, see Anita Haya Patterson, *From Emerson to King: Democracy, Race, and the Politics of Protest* (New York: Oxford University Press, 1997), 159–76.

53. Posnock, *Color and Culture,* 116.

54. For a description of the Jew who is willing to play the role of being "unlike the others" in exchange for economic mobility in post-emancipated Europe, see Hannah Arendt, *The Origins of Totalitarianism*, new ed. (New York: Harcourt, Brace, Jovanovich, 1973), particularly "The Jews and Society," chap. 3; and Arendt's *The Jew as Pariah: Jewish Identity and Politics in the Modern Age*, ed. Ron H. Feldman (New York: Grove Press, 1978), particularly "The Jew as Pariah: A Hidden Tradition," 67–95.

55. Du Bois's rejection of the "tragic mulatto" syndrome should not be construed as constituting an unwillingness to define himself as a mulatto. David Lewis states: "The subtext of proud hybridization is so prevalent in Du Bois's sense of himself that the failure to notice it in the literature about him is as remarkable as the complex itself." See Lewis, *W. E. B. Du Bois: Biography of a Race,* 148. In claiming that being a mulatto was a fundamental aspect of Du Bois's identity, Lewis led readers to believe that he would document how this self-identity manifested itself at various times in Du Bois's life. This did not occur.

56. According to Cornel West, in *The Souls of Black Folk* there are eighteen references to the cultural backwardness of black folks. See Cornel West, *The American Evasion of Philosophy,* 143–44.

57. Similar Herderian tensions between the folk and the man-of-culture are present in Ralph Ellison's understanding of the role of the Afro-American writer. See Jerry Gafio Watts, *Heroism and the Black Intellectual: Ralph Ellison, Politics, and Afro-American Intellectual Life* (Chapel Hill: University of North Carolina Press, 1994).

58. In his discussion of the sorrow songs, Du Bois matter-of-factly claims that the sentiments conveyed in one of the sorrow songs were similarly conveyed in a certain German folk song to which he quoted a line of the German lyrics. See Du Bois, *The Souls of Black Folk,* ed. Henry L. Gates, Jr., and Terri Hume Oliver (New York: Norton Critical Ed., 1998), 160.

59. Posnock, *Color and Culture,* 115–22. For Du Bois's embrace of pragmatism alone, see Cornel West, *The American Evasion of Philosophy,* 138–50.

60. For a historical overview of social Darwinism, see Mike Hawkins, *Social Darwinism in European and American Thought, 1860–1945: Nature as Model and Nature as Threat* (Cambridge: Cambridge University Press, 1997).

61. Du Bois, *The Souls of Black Folk* (Norton Critical Ed.), 59.

62. Du Bois, *The Souls of Black Folk* (Norton Critical Ed.), 68.

63. In 1921, Biddle University in Charlotte, North Carolina, changed its name to Johnson C. Smith University.

64. Du Bois, *The Souls of Black Folk* (Norton Critical Ed.), 68.

65. Du Bois, *The Souls of Black Folk* (Norton Critical Ed.), 69.

66. Du Bois, *The Souls of Black Folk* (Norton Critical Ed.), 69.

67. Transformative intellectuals are those who use their intellects in a critical fashion and do so by linking themselves to a social formation at-

tempting to gain power or influence for the subjugated. For a discussion of transformative intellectuals as a social formation, see Stanley Aronowitz and Henry A. Giroux, *Education under Siege: The Conservative, Liberal and Radical Debate over Schooling* (South Hadley, Mass.: Bergin and Garvey Publishers, 1985), 23–45.

68. As stated earlier, Du Bois must have been ambivalent about the existence of black women-of-culture. Yet, who more than Anna Julia Cooper deserved the designation "person-of-culture"? Unsurprisingly, the essay in *The Souls of Black Folk* that contains Du Bois's most explicit defense of the Negro's need for a liberal arts education is titled "On the Training of Black Men." Moreover, he accepted the exclusion of black women from the American Negro Academy. Why? See Moss, *The American Negro Academy.*

69. Du Bois, *The Souls of Black Folk,* 16–17.

70. There is a debate as to the significance of Hegelianism to Du Bois's "double-consciousness" formulation. Adolph Reed has argued that most scholars have grossly overstated the influence of Hegel on Du Bois. Instead of disproving the influence of Hegelianism on Du Bois, Reed presents arguments that document the existence of other strains of thought that used concepts of double consciousness that were prevalent in the United States at the time that Du Bois employed the concept. For some unexplained reason, Reed's attempt to contextualize Du Bois's notion of double consciousness within the intellectual currents of the time ignores Du Bois's schooling in Germany. See Reed, *W. E. B. Du Bois and American Political Thought: Fabianism and the Color Line* (New York: Oxford University Press, 1997), particularly chap. 7. A more convincing argument for the significance of Hegelianism to Du Bois's double-consciousness formulation is Zamir, *Dark Voices,* particularly chap. 4. For an additional discussion of Hegel's influence on Du Bois, see Williamson's *The Crucible of Race,* 399–413. See also Robert Gooding-Williams, "Philosophy of History and Social Critique in *The Souls of Black Folk,*" in *Social Science Information* 26, no. 1 (1987): 99–114; and Ross Posnock, *Color and Culture,* chap. 4.

71. For a rich interpretation of Hegel's "master-slave" discussion, see Alexander Kojeve's *Introduction to the Reading of Hegel,* ed. Allan Bloom, trans. James H. Nichols, Jr. (New York: Basic Books, 1969), chap. 2.

72. Zamir mentions that Du Bois probably read Hegel's *The Phenomenology of Mind* in a course taught by Professor George Santayana during the school year 1889–1900. See Zamir, *Dark Voices,* 113, 248–49. For an additional discussion of Du Bois's education at Harvard, see Arnold Rampersad, *The Art and Imagination of W. E. B. Du Bois* (Cambridge, Mass.: Harvard University Press, 1976), chap. 3.

73. For a description of Du Bois's pursuit of the doctorate in Germany, see Lewis, "Lehrjahre," *W. E. B. Du Bois: Biography of a Race,* chap. 6, 127–49. For a criticism of the first volume of the Lewis biography, see Sterling Stuckey, "The Tragedy of Scholarship: David Levering Lewis's

W. E. B. Du Bois," in *Souls: A Critical Journal of Black Politics, Culture and Society* 3, no. 2 (Spring 2001): 62–79.

74. An excellent overview of various ways that the Du Boisian idea of double consciousness has been interpreted by scholars is Ernest Allen, Jr., "On the Reading of Riddles: Rethinking Du Boisian Double Consciousness," in *Existence in Black: An Anthology of Black Existential Philosophy*, ed. Lewis R. Gordon (New York: Routledge, 1997), 49–68. Also see the special issue of *Contributions in Black Studies. A Journal of African and Afro-American Studies*, nos. 9/10 (1990–1992) concerning Du Bois's idea of double consciousness. In that special issue, three articles are vital to this discussion: Onita Estes-Hicks, "Cross-Cultural Explorations of Du Boisian Double-Consciousness: Jean Rhys and Jean Toomer," 6–16; Judith Wilson, "Lifting 'The Veil': Henry O. Tanner's The Banjo Lesson and The Thankful Poor," 31–54; and Ernest Allen, Jr., "Ever Feeling One's Twoness: 'Double Ideals' and 'Double Consciousness' in *The Souls of Black Folk*," 55–69.

75. *The Conservation of Races* was originally published as American Negro Academy Occasional Papers, No. 2, in 1897. It can also be found in Eric J. Sundquist, ed., *The Oxford W. E. B. Du Bois Reader* (New York: Oxford University Press, 1996), 38–47.

76. Kwame Anthony Appiah presents an argument for Du Bois as a racial essentialist in "Illusions of Race," in *In My Father's House: Africa in the Philosophy of Culture* (New York: Oxford University Press, 1992), chap. 2. For responses to Appiah, see Lucius Outlaw, "Conserve" Races? In Defense of W. E. B. Du Bois," and Robert Gooding-Williams, "Outlaw, Appiah, and Du Bois's 'The Conservation of Races,'" both of which appear in *W. E. B. Du Bois: On Race and Culture*, ed. Bernard Bell, Emily R. Grosholz, and James B. Stewart (New York: Routledge, 1996).

77. Zamir, *Dark Voices*, 116.

78. Du Bois has previously made this argument in *The Philadelphia Negro*, which was published in 1899. See "A Final Word," chap. 18.

79. For another discussion of the influence of Hegelianism on Du Bois's thought, see Paul Gilroy, *The Black Atlantic: Modernity and Double Consciousness* (Cambridge, Mass.: Harvard University Press, 1993), particularly chaps. 2 and 4.

80. Du Bois, *The Souls of Black Folk*, 52.

81. Du Bois, *The Souls of Black Folk*, 50.

82. Du Bois's exceptional Negro is caught in a state of hyperindividuality. He is not comfortably "at home" with either whites or blacks.

83. Rampersad, *The Art and Imagination of W. E. B. Du Bois*, 68.

84. Du Bois, *The Souls of Black Folk*, 112.

85. For example, I have no idea as to the quality of ideas contained in Cornel West's rap CD. Similarly, I cannot assess the degree to which he has mastered this popular culture art form. I do, however, sympathize with his desire to use an alternative medium in the hope of engaging a "different" black audience.

86. Horace Mann Bond, *Black American Scholars: A Study of Their Beginnings* (Detroit: Balamp Publishing, 1972), 26–28.

87. This lessening of deference to European culture has occurred within some disciplines more than others. For instance, comparative literature departments still view European literatures as the core components of their curriculum. The same could probably be said for philosophy departments. However, even within these disciplines, the beliefs and lives of "others" are taken into account more than at any previous moment in the American academy. Ironically, this more cosmopolitan outlook on the peoples of the world has been accompanied by a fetishization of European theories and theorists (e.g., Derrida, Lacan, Kristeva, Bourdieu). This fetishization has been central to many academic disciplines during the past twenty years.

88. While recently browsing through editions from the late 1930s through the early 1950s of the decidedly left-wing journal *Partisan Review,* I could not find any sustained criticism of the European colonial domination of African peoples.

89. Penny M. Von Eschen, *Race Against Empire: Black Americans and Anti-Colonialism, 1937–1957* (Ithaca, N.Y.: Cornell University Press, 1997), 17–18.

90. James H. Meriwether, *Proudly We Can Be Africans: Black Americans and Africa, 1935–1961* (Chapel Hill: University of North Carolina Press, 2002), 170–71.

91. Von Eschen, *Race Against Empire,* 175.

92. Robert H. Bates, V. Y. Mudimbe, and Jean O'Barr, eds., *Africa and the Disciplines: The Contributions of Research in Africa to the Social Sciences and Humanities* (Chicago: University of Chicago Press, 1993), 7.

93. Though many predominantly black colleges offered courses dealing with black life in America long before most predominantly white institutions, predominantly black colleges were slower than predominantly white colleges in establishing black studies programs/departments. Much of the reason for this hesitancy may be due to the conservative administrations at most black colleges. Another reason was a simple shortage of funding. See Henry N. Drewry and Humphrey Doermann, *Stand and Prosper: Private Black Colleges and Their Students* (Princeton, N.J.: Princeton University Press, 2001), 111–14.

94. Hall, *In the Vineyard: Working in African American Studies* (Knoxville: University of Tennessee Press, 1999); Manning Marable, ed., *Dispatches from the Ebony Tower: Intellectuals Confront the African American Experience* (New York: Columbia University Press, 2000); and Johnnella E. Butler, ed., *Color-Line to Borderlands: The Matrix of American Ethnic Studies* (Seattle: University of Washington Press, 2001), particularly the essay by Rhett S. Jones, "From Ideology to Institution: The Evolution of Africana Studies," 113–49.

95. According to Drewry and Doermann, prior to World War II most scholarly research on black history and culture had been carried out at private black colleges. Following World War II, the center of research on

black life was no longer the private black college. See *Stand and Prosper,* 112. Insofar as black scholars would not be hired at white colleges until twenty years after the end of World War II, where was research on black history/culture centered? At predominantly black public institutions? At federally funded Howard University?

96. See Jill Quadagno, *The Color of Welfare: How Racism Undermined the War on Poverty* (New York: Oxford University Press, 1994); David Zucchino, *The Myth of the Welfare Queen* (New York: Scribner, 1997); Martin Gilens, *Why Americans Hate Welfare: Race, Media and the Politics of Anti-Poverty Policies* (Chicago: University of Chicago Press, 2001); and Ange-Marie Hancock, *The Politics of Disgust: The Public Identity of the Welfare Queen* (New York: New York University Press, 2004).

97. The idea of a utilitarian imperative is simple. For our purposes, utilitarianism means maximizing the greatest benefits for the largest number of people. Imperative means that individuals feel this as a mandatory, utterly necessary duty. As such, a utilitarian imperative is simply the sense that an individual has a duty to act in a way that maximizes benefits to his or her community (in this instance, the black community).

98. I invoke the term *utilitarian imperative* to refer to the process whereby an individual constructs her intellectual/scholarly agendas (i.e., goals of graduate study; research subjects) on the basis of a desire to materially benefit a designated community such as an ethnic group, race, or gender. An intellectual who is governed by a utilitarian imperative allows the external needs of her community or society to dictate her areas of intellectual inquiry. Moreover, such an intellectual feels the need to be of service to a designated community or goal. In many respects, the utilitarian imperative is but a desire to make her intellect function in a socially useful, instrumental fashion. Needless to say, an intellectual's social utility is usually determined by the potential changes in the material circumstances of a designated group that could accrue from her work.

99. The quotation is taken from the essay "The Dilemma of the Black Intellectual" in Cornel West, *Keeping Faith: Philosophy and Race in America* (New York: Routledge, 1993), 75.

100. Woodson makes a similar economic utilitarian argument for black education in his now classic 1933 polemic, *Mis-education of the Negro* (Washington, D.C.: Associated Publishers, 1969).

101. General Samuel Armstrong was a northern white supremacist who advocated explicitly reactionary racial policies for the South. See James D. Anderson, *The Education of Blacks in the South, 1860–1935* (Chapel Hill: University of North Carolina Press, 1988), particularly "The Hampton Model of Normal School Industrial Education, 1868–1915," chap. 2.

102. Booker T. Washington, *Up From Slavery* (New York: Signet Classic, 2000), 85.

103. Anderson, *The Education of Blacks in the South, 1860–1935,* chap. 2.

Index

Abolition Society and Friends, 49
academic disciplines, 44, 146–47*n*3
accommodationism, 12, 18, 91,
  105, 155*n*26
acculturation, 111, 122, 123
A.C. McClurg and Company, 19,
  22
ACOA. *See* American Committee
  on Africa (ACOA)
Africa, social research on, 30
African Americans, 19, 51;
  approaches to investigation of,
  44, 147*n*4; attitudes toward,
  100–101; better element of,
  103–4; characteristics of,
  102–3; as characterized by
  Basset, 139*n*39; essay on life of,
  119–21; existential dimensions
  of empirical methods of research
  of, 52–61, 149*nn*21–22;
  methodological approaches to
  existential dimensions of, 48–52,
  148–49*nn*11–13, 149*n*16; social
  advancement of, 46–48; as
  social category, 43, 143–45*n*1;
  stereotypes of white Americans,
  64. *See also* black Americans
African American women, agency
  of, 3, 31
Africanize America, 120–21
African studies, 128–29, 162*n*93
African Studies Association, 128
*Africa: Toward a History of the
  Continent*, 27
Afro-American studies, 128–29,
  162*n*93, 162–63*n*95
agency, of African American
  women, 3, 31; color prejudice
  as, 67
Allen, Ernest, Jr., 64, 148*n*7

American Committee on Africa
  (ACOA), 128
American Journal of Sociology, 22
*American Monthly Review of
  Reviews*, 22
American Negro Academy, 16, 101
The American Negro Family, 30,
  31, 35–36, 141*n*4
American Society of African
  Culture (AMSAC), 128
American Sociological Association,
  3
AMSAC. *See* American Society of
  African Culture (AMSAC)
anarchy, 77
Andrews, Tina, 142*n*26
anticolonialism, 127–28
Appiah, Anthony, 11, 151*n*52
Aptheker, Herbert, 13, 26, 27,
  140*n*58
Armstrong, Samuel, 134, 163*n*101
Arnold, Matthew, 77, 112
artists, and the white world, 97–98
Atlanta Compromise, 17, 93
Atlanta University, 14, 18, 141*n*5;
  appointment as professor, 16;
  and Du Bois's research, 105; and
  publication of *Souls*, 21; Study
  of Negro Problems conference,
  30
Atlantic Monthly, 147*n*5
*The Autobiography of W.E.B. Du
  Bois*, 27, 140*n*58

Baker, Houston, 112
Baldwin, James, 98, 100
Baraka, Amiri, 98
Barnett, Ferdinand, 24
Basset, John Spencer, 22, 128*n*39
Bell, Daniel, 100

About the Authors

Elizabeth Higginbotham is currently Professor in the Department of Sociology at the University of Delaware. She is a native New Yorker who did her undergraduate work at City College of CUNY and graduate work at Brandeis University. Higginbotham is the author of *Too Much to Ask: Black Women in the Era of Integration* (University of North Carolina Press 2001) and coeditor of *Women and Work: Exploring Race, Ethnicity, and Class* (Sage 1997) and *Race and Ethnicity in Society: The Changing Landscape* (Thomson-Wadsworth 2006). Her articles appear in *Gender & Society, Women's Studies Quarterly,* and many edited collections.

Charles Lemert is Andrus Professor of Sociology at Wesleyan University and author of many books, including *Durkheim's Ghosts: Cultural Logics and Social Things* (Cambridge University Press 2006), *Deadly Worlds: The Emotional Costs of Globalization* (with Anthony Elliott, Rowman & Littlefield 2005), *Muhammad Ali: Trickster in the Culture of Irony* (Polity Press 2004), *Dark Thoughts: Race and the Eclipse of Society* (Routledge 2002), and the third edition of his best-selling text, *Social Things: An Introduction to the Sociological Life* (Rowman & Littlefield 2005).

Manning Marable is Professor of Public Affairs, History, and African-American Studies and director of the Center for Contemporary Black History at Columbia University. He is the author of *Great Wells of Democracy* (Basic Books 2003) and *W. E. B. Du Bois: Black Radical Democrat,* updated edition (Paradigm 2004).

Jerry G. Watts is Professor of English at the Graduate Center of CUNY. He is the author of *Heroism and the Black Intellectual: Ralph Ellison, Politics, and Afro-American Intellectual Life* (University of North Carolina Press 1994) and *Amiri Baraka: The Politics and Art of a Black Intellectual* (NYU Press 2001) and editor of Harold Cruse's *The Crisis of the Negro Intellectual: Reconsidered* (Routledge 2004).

Alford A. Young, Jr., is Arthur F. Thurnau Professor and Associate Professor of Sociology in the Center for Afro-American and African Studies at the University of Michigan. He is the author of *The Minds of Marginalized Black Men: Making Sense of Mobility, Opportunity, and Future Life Chances* (Princeton University Press 2004) as well as articles on the African American urban experience and African American social theory in *Sociological Theory, The Annual Review of Sociology,* and other journals.